Love, Life and Hope

C J Ford

Love, Life and Hope

Actions Speak Louder Than Words

C J Ford

To order additional copies of this book, contact:
Xlibris
1-888-795-4274
www.Xlibris.com
Orders@Xlibris.com
548701

LISTING OF STORIES

FOREWORD

Love, Life and Hope, ….. What is important to write in the forward to this book? Do I index the book into separate sections of 'Love and Life' / 'Life and Hope'/ 'Love and Hope?' Different sections that gives something to all people?….Or do I just leave it written as one long story of my experiences??

…… The most important thing seems to be that anyone and everyone who reads this book will now have a deeper understanding of their own life.

Thoughts for the forward to this book…….. To all men everywhere I seek to bring understanding and joy to your life both now and later. To men and women of all thoughts and beliefs I would that you find something important to yourself from my experience, as a parallel to your own life experience that you may discover a greater happiness in your own life. ….This is my perspective on *love, life and hope*. …..Show Love first whenever you can, because Life itself, gives us Hope. You may have an even better perspective than I. Because of my experiences I have better than I used to have. If we have a better perspective than some others do we can encourage them. I write this with a desire to help everyone understand better the giving of love and the love of giving.

Ask yourself, if you knew your life would be 'upside down' tomorrow, what would you do different today. ……Today is the only day we have. …….Live today with a perspective of love.

…..This book is not written just to those who say they believe in God, it is written to the sad and lonely and those looking for hope regardless of what they believe. Look for the evidence of joy and brotherly love in people's actions, and not only in the words they speak. Anyone can speak grand words, but it is the actions of those words that have lasting value.

What additional thoughts would I write in a forward to the book......?..... *'This is written to all people, my thoughts and my feelings, my beliefs and my actions.'*

Hopefully the understanding I have been given, contained in this book, can draw people together in love, in both the realm of human relationships to each other, and spiritually, to a deeper, and ultimately, a full understanding of God's greater Love for each of us as well.

It is my desire through this book to see all men and women drawn to a more appreciative relationship to others, and to each other in each our personal lives and to help each person reading this book to gain a better insight into my personal perspective, and understanding of the Love I have for my God and my Savior...... not just my belief in God.... My Love for Him and all that He has done for me.

LOVE LIFE & HOPE
Actions Speak Louder Than Words
C J Ford

The writing of this book did not start out as a plan to write a book. Many little things and circumstances all contributed to one day starting to write down each day's thoughts of my heart on a piece of paper carried in my pocket, the collection of which has now become the book: *Love, Life, and Hope.*

Arrival In Norway

The thoughts, inspiration, and understanding now revealed in the pages of this book began with the decision that I needed to take a walk alone up to the top of the mountain on Aspøya, (ahsp'-oye-ah) an island on the western coast of Norway, where just a few days earlier I had come to live for the summer months.

I had been coming here for both the winter and summer months for many years. My trips to Norway for the previous 13 years were always exciting and fun filled.

What was different this Sunday summer evening was that in the past months of the previous year I had lost the precious love of my life, Alicia. To most people it would have appeared as the simple breakup of a relationship.

Many people would say, and some did say, "Forget her, get over it, get on with your life and find someone new." But for me, the absence of Alicia's presence in my life was an emptiness, a lonesomeness, and a loneliness that I had never experienced in my life before now.

I was sitting in the living room of my friend's home after we had finished supper, and while I was trying to focus on the conversation with my friends, thoughts of Alicia and her absence dominated the thoughts in my mind and weighed heavily upon my heart.

All of my life I had always enjoyed good conversation on any and every topic, but now that Sunday evening June 20, 2010, I found myself just wanting to be alone, physically alone with no one to interrupt my thoughts of the wonderful memories of Alicia and her son Marc's trip to Norway to visit here almost one year earlier than that Sunday evening.

Fjelltur

So, for an excuse to have that intimate privacy with my thoughts, I told my friends that I thought I would take a fjelltur ('feyell-toour'/mountain trip) up Vettafjell ('vetta-feyell') and maybe I would even stay overnight up at their cabin on the mountain. They said "Fine, see you later, have a good trip." I packed up some bread and cheese and took some apples with, not sure how long I would be up there.

It was about 1 mile to walk from the farm to the base of the mountain where people usually drove to and started walking from. Even at a slow walk, the mile passed quickly as I thought about last year with Alicia and Marc here, and I soon found myself walking into the forest on a small Skogs Vei ('ssKogs vay',) a forest road just wide enough for a small tractor, made and used for forest work.

As I came to the first fork in the road, I deliberately took the 'wrong way,' the path straight ahead instead of the path to the right, which was the easier path to follow to the mountaintop.

Just one year earlier, the first week of July 2009, Alicia and Marc came to Norway for two weeks to visit me. Alicia had wanted Marc to experience the same beauty of the nature in Norway that she and I had experienced the previous February, when Alicia and I had climbed this same mountain together. I chose now not to take just a fjelltur, but to retrace as closely as possible the path that Marc, Alicia and I had walked together.

I had accidentally taken the 'wrong path' to start with the summer before with Alicia and Marc, and we soon found ourselves with no path. I was a little confused, but did not say anything because I did not want Alicia to feel afraid. I was not lost, just the trail was lost. I knew I was off the beaten path, but I also knew that I had to be just to the right or left of the normally traveled path, because I could see Tingvoll fjord off to my left and knew that all I needed to do was to just keep going straight up the mountain and we would get to where we wanted to go.

We had taken the path to a small hill to the left of the path where we should have gone, and I realized that when we came to the 'top' of the small hill and had to go down again and to the right, where we found the well-traveled and worn footpath.

Feeling a little less 'Lost in the Woods,' Alicia wanted to stop and rest a bit and just look out at the view of the fjords and distant mountains that were just beginning to appear.

Marc was more anxious to quickly get going, so when we started walking again, Marc ran ahead of us far enough that Alicia called out to him worried that he would get lost. He waited for us to catch up and said he wanted to run ahead to the top of the mountain on his own.

I told Alicia he could not get lost because the path goes straight to the mountaintop. Marc agreed to stay following the path keeping Tingvoll fjord in view to his left, and Alicia agreed to let him go ahead by himself.

Marc excitedly took off on his own with his newfound freedom and independence. As he ran up the mountain, Alicia and I watched him disappear and reappear between the trees. Alicia excitedly exclaimed "Look at him go!! ...He never runs like that at home, and his asthma doesn't even seem to bother him here!!"

Even as Marc disappeared out of sight, I felt like he was still right there with Alicia and me. We were like a family doing something special together. All three of us filled with joyfulness and a easiness in our hearts. As Alicia and I shared our happiness for Marc's happiness, I enjoyed the wonderful pleasure of Alicia's presence as we walked together.

I hold fast to the memory of walking with and being in the presence of the most important person in the world to me. ....The most important person in the world. ..... How does someone achieve that level of importance in your life?

How We Met

Alicia and I had only 'met' nine months earlier. Alicia had connected with me through a Yahoo Personals ad. Alicia's info said that she was tall, slender, and she worked in the medical field. She liked to eat healthy, organic if possible, but was not obsessed with it, and she had no picture posted.

I liked everything that she had written about herself, but what in addition caught my interest the most was that she said she went to church weekly, and was looking for someone that went weekly, or more than once a week. ... I thought to myself... *There may be a reason for that.*

So I answered her request for an e-mail from me together with my cell phone number. Alicia replied with an e-mail and her cell phone number, and said that she too would rather talk than write.

Alicia was the first to call me the following day. As she identified herself we started to visit about general things. For the first five minutes or so, I was just visiting with an interesting newfound acquaintance, but as we talked, I quickly acquired a serious interest in our conversation as we each discussed our personal interests and values.

Our first phone conversation lasted more than 45 minutes, and after we hung up, I said out loud, "Lord, I want to meet this woman, and *I don't care if she's butt ugly.*" Something special about Alicia and the feelings of her heart came clearly through to me on that first phone call.

The next day I returned home about 11 p.m. after the day's work. I checked my e-mail as usual and Alicia had sent me a picture of herself that I thought looked like it had been taken 20 years earlier, since I knew we were both the same age of 55.

I thought, if she looked that pretty 20 years ago, she probably still looks ok. But as I looked into her eyes in the picture, because she had been looking directly into the camera, it seemed as if I was looking into her heart. Even in her picture, somehow in her eyes, together with her pleasant smile, I thought I saw the '*Something that I had been looking for.*'

I just sat there at the desk in my office staring at her picture, and suddenly started laughing joyfully as I said out loud, "Lord! I might be looking at a picture of my wife!" I sent off an e-mail and said that I thought her picture looked like she was 38, or 37 maybe! ...... Then I heard nothing more for the next four days, and her site disappeared.

I started to think that maybe she had been in a car accident or something, and she doesn't look like that now. I was afraid I had hurt her feelings or somehow insulted her and she had blocked me from her site.

The following Sunday morning I was driving to the restaurant for coffee thinking about which church I wanted to go to that morning.

I decided to call Alicia and ask her where she went to church and if it would be okay if I came to her church to meet her. She said "I go to Bethany Evangelical Free in La Crosse, Where are you now?" I said, "I am in Viroqua, about an hour away from there." She said, "I am just ready to go to the nine o'clock service, but I will wait and meet you in the hallway for the 10:30 service."

I skipped my coffee and drove straight to the church, arriving about 10:15. I walked through the upstairs and downstairs hallways, greeting any of the taller ladies I passed, not sure what Alicia would look like, different from the picture that she had sent me.

Then I saw her in the upstairs hallway in the middle of a crowd. She was only about 20 feet away from me, tightly packed into the crowd of people that were filling into the hallway just before services would start.

Her face had blended in with all the other people, and it was only the moment that her eyes caught mine, that I knew it was her. We never broke our gaze into each other's eyes as we walked toward each other, and as I felt that I had looked into her heart through her eyes, I said in my thoughts, *"Lord, I am done looking."*

I put out my hand to greet her and she pulled me into her and gave me a hug. I was not expecting that and was not prepared for the emotional experience that accompanied it.

For the past few days, I had been feeling unsure why I had not heard from her, and why had her site disappeared?

For the past hour, because she had welcomed me to come to her church, I had been holding her in my heart, and now I was holding her in my arms.

In those few moments I found the contentment of the heart that I had been searching for.

Contentment of the heart......It is what each of us wants from life, isn't it. We sat together that morning as comfortable as if we had been together for years.

When the service was over, I asked her if she would like to join me for dinner; and I knew her answer would be yes.

After finishing our meal we were only some minutes into our conversation when I said, "Alicia, I think you are a wonderful woman and I really like you, but I am not interested in dating you, I am interested in getting married to you." "I feel the same way" was her immediate reply.

Something wonderful transpired in those moments looking directly into each other's eyes and hearts. Words were not necessary. I had essentially just asked Alicia to marry me less than three hours after meeting her, and she had responded affirmatively.

Our conversation continued with an easy flow of words, talking together with the mindset of a certain future together. I do not remember now everything we discussed that Sunday afternoon, but I remember in general we talked about anything and everything.

I was so totally focused on the conversation between Alicia and me that I was unaware of whoever else was at the restaurant. I realized that the moment one of my farmer neighbors and friend Kevin walked up to our table and said "Hi Curt." I said 'Hi' back to him and said "I didn't even see you here."

Kevin said "Ya, I saw you walk by a couple times and you didn't see me so I thought I would stop by your table and say hi." I then said, "Kevin, I would like you to meet my friend Alicia, Alicia, this is one of my friends Kevin, and one of Kevin's sisters is married to one of my cousins"

I felt a bit awkward and restrained introducing Alicia as only my friend to Kevin, knowing that the longer and longer we visited she had become so much more important to me than just another good friend.

I remember calling my sister Diane who lived only a few minutes' drive from the steakhouse we were at and asked her if I could stop over, as I was with someone I would like her and Peter to meet. She said they were out of town, and we could do it another time.

Yes, we could do it another time. There would be plenty of time, a lifetime. I was excited to begin introducing this truly wonderful and special woman to all of my family and friends.

I had found the fulfillment in my heart that I had so long searched for. I had found what my Grandmother Nora had told me about as a young teenager, "When you find the right one, you will know. I can't tell you how or why, but you will just know it." Now I knew exactly what she was talking about.

Like our first phone call that quickly became nearly an hour visit, this first Sunday afternoon passed before we knew it, and only when a car's headlights were turned on outside of the window next to our table, did I realize that nearly five hours had passed since we had finished eating dinner. We were both a little surprised that we had not even noticed that the daylight had turned to darkness.

As we left the restaurant our hands soon found each other's. Our fingers clasped firmly and yet gently together as we walked at a comfortable pace, in no particular hurry to reach our cars parked on the outside row across the parking lot.

As we reached the driver's side of Alicia's car, we turned toward each other and still holding hands from walking together, our free hands soon found their place with each other and now my other hand was enjoying the same pleasure of Alicia's gentle touch. As we stood there I thanked Alicia for the wonderful day, not wanting to let go of her hands.

Only as we agreed that it was time to get going did we let go of our hand hold for an even more wonderful embrace. It was a special kind of hug that was a combination of emotions for me, the blend of a firm embrace of saying goodbye to a loved one as they prepare to board a flight, not certain when you will see them again, and also the comfortable easy embrace of saying goodbye to a loved one in the morning as they leave for the day's work, expecting to see them home for supper.

It reminded me wonderfully of the first hug Alicia had given me that morning in the church hallway. The only thing that was different now, was that I was prepared for, anticipating, and eagerly looking forward to her wonderful embrace, now fully able to enjoy the closeness in the blending together of each our personal space.

We lingered longer than the few moments of that morning's first embrace. I enjoyed also knowing that there were more hugs waiting in our future.

The thought crossed my mind to kiss her good night, and I knew that would have taken us over the top. I chose instead to give her a gentle kiss on her right cheek where mine had been resting, saving the anticipation of that first kiss for a more special place than the parking lot.

Those Who Hold An Important Place In Our Life

As I walked here now alone on the mountain, it was not the wonderful beginning days of our relationship that were on my mind, it was the completeness that Alicia and Marc had brought into my life, the security in my heart and the certainty that I felt for the future. Although I have many interests and responsibilities in life, they had become my No. 1 priority.

It was not just Alicia's presence and companionship that I longed for, it was Alicia's, *AND* Marc's presence. Somehow Marc had stolen my heart also. Somehow Marc made my relationship to Alicia even more complete for me, more satisfying and brought a deeper sense of contentment and oneness.

As I passed through this area on the mountain where Alicia and I had enjoyed seeing Marc take off on his own venture to the mountaintop, it seemed now symbolic in my memory of parents having raised a child up from infancy and now watched together as he successfully ventured out confidently on his own, spreading his wings, and for the first time, leaping out from the security of the nest into the open air beneath.

It has been written, *'And the two shall become one.'* When a man and a woman bare a child together, truly, 'the two have become one.' They have together now created one anew who has become 'one Mind, one Body, and one Spirit.' Some children are physically born to a couple and some are adopted. To some people on the outside of the family looking in, they see one child as the couple's 'own' and another child as the 'adopted' one.

To the parents of either or both, they are the same, and while I have one son from my first marriage, whom I love dearly together with my daughter-in-law and three grandchildren. Marc had entered into the same realm for me, becoming like my son also, born not of the flesh, but born of the heart, an extension of my love and compassion for Alicia. Marc somehow became a fulfillment for me in my heart of my love for Alicia, a feeling of a greater connection for me of a shared and multiplied love for each other.

My son Chris is a permanent connection to his mother forever, and likewise the love I found in my heart for Marc feels like a permanent connection to Alicia's heart; I have felt and experienced a common love, devotion, and commitment to Marc.

My love for each Marc and Alicia was experienced symbolically for me at mealtime in Alicia's home when the three of us grasped each other's hands, as we bowed our heads to give thanks for our blessings and the food before us. In those few moments we also connected as a family in a special way for me.

When three people hold hands in a triangle, each is connected to the other equally. If any two of the three let go of their hand hold, each person still has a connection through the one in between. The three can now walk together in harmony. When three hearts walk together in joyful harmony, the contentment is the same whether you are holding hands or not. A child can be a common link that can restore a mother and father's broken marriage or relationship. Sometimes it is a common friend that can restore a broken friendship. Perhaps you, my book reader friend, can do this for two of your common friends, each of us doing our part as often as we can to make our lives and our world a better place for all of us.

Reliving A Special Experience

As the mountain path narrowed now before me, I thought back to when Alicia had to go in front of me because there was not enough room on the path to walk side by side. I was content to follow behind her watching her choices of where to step.

The path had become steep in places, a combination of protruding rocks and tree roots which had now become like a stairway up the steeper embankments. The foot traffic of both people and animals had left a well-worn trail through the grass and other small plants of the forest. Rain over time had washed away the soil from the tops of stones and the small tree roots that crisscrossed the trail under the surface. The roots now lay exposed holding back the soil that lay behind them having leveled out with the tops of the roots revealing an ideal stairway.

As Alicia and I encountered these short stretches of the steeper pathway, I followed closely behind her choosing the same rocks and roots to step on while I was unable to walk beside her. I was following exactly in her footsteps, until I was able to join by her side on the path ahead.

As I now walked alone thinking back to those moments I had followed Alicia so closely, I chose my footsteps carefully wondering which of the roots I stepped on had been graced by the touch of Alicia's foot.

It did not matter now if I walked slowly or quickly, I was alone. There was no motivation to get to where I was going quickly, because when I arrived, I would still be alone.

Jeremy And Izzy

The thoughts of my heart now turned away from my sadness to the heavy sorrow and emptiness in the lives of another family back in the states. Only three weeks earlier I had attended the funeral of a young father and his 3-year-old daughter who had been tragically killed in a head-on collision.

Returning from a trip to Portland, Oregon and Vancouver, BC, I had stopped at a coffee shop in Minnesota as I neared home.

Glancing through the local paper, I read about the tragic account of a young father who on the previous Saturday morning had taken his 3-year-old daughter and 11-month-old son to the local library for children's story time. Returning home afterward they met a vehicle pulling a trailer, of which the trailer came unhooked from the truck pulling it, hitting the pavement causing it to cross the centerline, crashing head-on into the young father's vehicle killing him and his little daughter instantly, and amazingly, somehow his infant son in the back seat was spared.

As I read the article, I learned of the young father's community service as a fireman, first responder, library board of director's activities and his devotion to taking his daughter and son to Saturday morning story time at the library. I read that the little girl Isabel, called 'Izzy,' loved to dress up in special little dresses for public celebrations and had learned to count to 10 in Norwegian.

All of a sudden, instantly, the tragedy of this family's loss gripped my heart. The young father Jeremy was 32 years old, only a few years younger than my son Chris, and little Izzy was only a couple of years younger than my own granddaughter Allison, who is called 'Allie.' I had also taught Allie to count to 10 in Norwegian. The younger of my two grandsons Brayden, was also only a couple years older than Jeremy's son Liam, who had survived the accident.

As I sat sipping my coffee in silence, my heart pondered the sorrow and emptiness in the life of the young mother left alone with only her young son to hold in her arms, never to hold her daughter or husband again.

Life as she had known it…shattered forever; and the parents of the young man having lost a child also, even though he was a grown man.

I also thought of both sets of grandparents losing a grandchild, and the grandparents who lost a son-in-law who becomes like a son, the father of your grandchild.

Jeremy and Izzy had been torn from their families in a moment of time, no warning, no preparation, and no explanation for what had occurred.

Time stops for those left behind. You do not know when or how to take the next step, or where it will lead; I just sat there reading and re-reading the article, not knowing why. I kept reading it over and over, until my coffee had gone stone cold.

People who were unknown to me and strangers only an hour earlier, now seized the feelings of my heart with their tragic loss, and then I realized that my loss of Marc and Alicia from my life was just as sudden and tragic for me. They were gone from my presence and my life, seemingly without warning. I understood the feelings and emotions that each of

Jeremy's and Izzy's family members were going through; the unexplainable questions of how and why this had happened.

It only took me a moment more to know that I had already automatically made a decision that I needed to go to the funeral visitation that was scheduled for them, just to let the family know that their loss had touched even the life of a stranger to them, and to let them know that I was sharing the burden of their sorrow and holding them in my prayers. Their hopes and dreams for the present and the future were gone, never to return. Cast as a heavy stone into the darkest depths of the ocean, never again to see the light of day.

I had been feeling like this over my loss of Marc and Alicia. I had been living a life of sorrow, filled with grief, grieving, and despair. All my hopes, dreams, and plans for our future had vanished into thin air, like the early morning mist in the air that vanishes before your eyes and you can do nothing to stop it.

So had my hope been fading, until it hung by barely a thread, but a thread it was...it was still hanging by a thread because Alicia and Marc were still here living life in a parallel to mine. This gave my heart some measure of peace and comfort to my hope, reinforcing and strengthening the thread of hope that ran through my heart, trusting that it was as strong as good fishing line and able to endure the tests of strength that may lie ahead. I had to go on in the spirit of hope, even if alone. Jeremy and Izzy's family had to go on living, even though Jeremy and Izzy were not.

I arrived at the visitation for them at the earliest scheduled time. Already there was a line of people all the way out onto the sidewalk and across the lawn to the street. I took my place at the end of this line of strangers to me, acknowledging the people near me with only a nod of the head and an occasional soft hello. Few people had much of anything to say to anyone.

I had only stood in line for a few minutes when I heard, "Hello Curt." I turned around to see two of my good friends from this community, Larry and his wife Charlene. I said "Hi" to them, looked them both in the eye and just shook my head sideways from left to right a couple of times, and we said little of anything more.

The solemnity from within the church extended out well beyond the churchyard into the street, where even the cars were approaching slower than normal.

When I finally entered the church corridor, I beheld Jeremy and Izzy's life laid out before me in pictures of life and happiness; Jeremy's fireman's suit and other material things from their life together, a Mother's Day card from Jeremy to the Love of his life Kristie, in which Jeremy expressed the gratefulness and joy he held in his heart for his wife and their blessings, a picture of Jeremy lying down with his precious little girl lying close by his side in perfect peace and contentment, safe and secure in her father's arms.

As I read the cards and looked at the majority of the pictures, each photo revealed for me a deeper appreciation of Jeremy's love for his family. I came to feel that I personally knew Jeremy and little Izzy, and there were so many parallels to my own son and his family.

I had looked at so many pictures and things laid out representing Jeremy and Izzy's life that I had completely lost my place in line. The people I walked in with were now coming back out of the church and I realized that when I saw Larry and Charlene come back into the hallway.

Time was irrelevant and it seemed that I had only been looking at the pictures and things for a few moments, yet dozens of people had went through past me, talked with the family, and returned to the church hallway.

As I now entered the church and followed the line of people as they progressed forward, there was only a quiet murmur of conversation coming from the front of the church. The blending together of the sounds of many individual conversations as each of the visitors softly offered their condolences and sympathy to each of Jeremy and Izzy's remaining family members, simultaneously resulting in a quiet hum of conversation.

Strangely absent from the sounds of everything was the absence of any sounds of crying from where I stood. I wondered if they were just all cried out and couldn't cry anymore? The answer to that question came as it became my turn to speak with the family members.

As I put out my hand and offered my sympathy to this young widowed mother Kristie, she said to me, "And who are you now?" "I am a complete stranger to you" was my reply, "I am from Wisconsin and I was returning home from a trip, when I stopped for coffee in Hokah yesterday where I read about Jeremy and Izzy's accident in the newspaper. The more I read the newspaper the more my heart went out to you and your family and your burden of sorrow in your loss of Jeremy and Izzy. I have a son and a little granddaughter also and I knew that I just had to come and let you and your family know that your sorrow is shared even by people that don't know you."

Kristie responded with "Thank you for letting me know that. We appreciate everyone that has come. We don't know why this has happened, but we trust that God has a reason for allowing it to happen even if we don't understand it now. Jeremy and Izzy both loved Jesus as their Savior and we know they're happy and safe in Heaven with him now."

Now, I understood....... I now understood the absence of crying when I entered the church sanctuary. As it is written, *'We sorrow, yet not as others sorrow who have no hope.'* I understood fully the hope, and at least a measure of the peace of mind that Kristie possessed that made it possible for her to endure this present sorrow that had beset her and her family.

I thought back to 34 years earlier when late in the night on the 3rd of May 1976, on my 23rd birthday, when in the space of a few moments of time, I had acquired this same understanding, assurance and peace of mind.

It humbled me now to witness and observe the strength this young widowed mother had, mingled together with the deep sorrow in her heart of Jeremy and Izzy's absence from this life. Kristie expressed a confidence that her dear little Izzy was safe and happy in her father's arms as they went together to meet Jesus.

As I moved on to speak with each of Jeremy and Kristie's parents, they mirrored Kristie's acceptance of what they could not change, while also embracing that same hope and confidence that Kristie held in her heart.

The absence of Jeremy and Izzy from this physical life would change forever the future for each of the family members. What seemed most important to me was that each of their lives had already been filled to overflowing with blessings because of the presence of Jeremy and Izzy in their lives here. The precious memories of Jeremy and Izzy would now last forever, existing parallel alongside their physical absence.

Treasured Memories

I could now relate to how my life had been similarly changed by Alicia and Marc for me. All I had to hold onto for the present was all the good memories that I held in my heart of the one full and wonderful year with Alicia and Marc a part of it.

A year so fully wonderful and complete for me that it seemed now that Alicia had always been a part of my life, because she was the fulfillment of all that my heart had searched for; and as I grew to know Marc, I did not know then that I would also embrace him in love as my own son in my heart, later one day on the edge of a high mountain cliff.

Because of so abruptly losing Alicia and Marc out of my daily life, I could seemingly relate fully and completely with the unpredictable sudden absence of Jeremy and Izzy to their families and the sudden loss of someone or anyone you love dearly. Death is separation. The pain of their absence is the same in death, divorce, or the severance of a relationship. You cannot go somewhere to be in their presence and experience again the joy you once knew.

It is the reason we all are compelled to do the only thing we can do, on whichever occasions that are important to us in our memory. We can visit again special places where joyfulness and happiness was shared, or perhaps bring flowers, or a flower to the final resting place of a special loved one.

Even though they are no longer physically present, standing on a special place, or placing flowers or a flower by a gravestone, we are closer to the memories we all hold in our hearts of those we have loved.......... Even if it is only for a moment or two, standing there we are as close as we can get to the memories we have stored up in our heart, and we can fully experience in our memory the special moments we shared with them while they were here with us.

One Breath Of Air At A Time

Those moments of joyful memories can be as important to us as a breath of fresh air to a drowning man. It does not matter when or where the next breath of air will come from, it was THe breath of air we needed right now in the present moment that was what mattered .....for now. It buys a little time. Maybe just one breath of air is all it takes for us to make it back on top of the water where we can survive.

Perhaps that was what my fjelltur now was all about for me, physically going somewhere and doing something that brought me back into the experience of the wonderful memories of life with Alicia and Marc a part of it.

Little did I know at the time that day, as the three of us climbed the mountain together, that later that same day I would experience, together with Alicia and Marc, the greatest physical and emotional joyfulness in laughter I had ever known in my life.

Walking alone up the mountain now, I held at least a thread of hope in my heart that there was, a chance, of a chance, of a chance that we could find and live that joyful experience together again. The three of us had entered the forest together enjoying all the beauty and majesty the nature in Norway holds.

As much as I enjoyed the three of us hiking up the mountain together, I also appreciated Marc wanting to go ahead on his own, leaving Alicia and I alone together to experience the warmth of the summer air and the wonderful smells of the forest.

Quite different from our fjelltur the previous winter when the fragrance of pine trees filled the cool, crisp mountain air, and firewood from that same type of tree warmed the cabin with a fragrance all its own.

Winter or summer, inside or out in nature's creation, in a Palace or a Hut, Alicia's very presence was always the centerpiece of my joy.

I needed a breath of fresh air to survive. I had unexpectedly experienced the wind knocked out of me in losing Alicia out of my life with the unexplainable events that had occurred just a little over six months earlier. My heart was still breaking, and I was struggling to make sense of it.

A New Church

Alicia had told me about a great new Church she was attending and one day I thought I would just go attend one of the Sunday morning services to see for myself.

When looking up the address for the church I thought she was going to in her home town, I noticed the name to a small community Bible Church that seemed to stand out in the phone book from all the other Churches, in another town away from where Alicia lived. I said to the Lord in my thoughts, *"OK Lord, I will go to Alicia's Church today and the Bible Church next Sunday and offer to sing a song for their service."*

The Bible Church and Pastor Jim's sermon left a big impact on me in many respects and I returned the following Wednesday night for a men's Bible study.

Pastor Jim, who had warmly welcomed me the past Sunday, was then angry with me and said that Alicia was attending his church and when she arrived and saw my car, she returned home, calling him later and said she thought that I was following her.

I left to go back home that Wednesday night a bit sad for the misunderstandings, I felt that I had just lost a newfound friend. I learned later that Pastor Jim had called Alicia that night after I left and told her 'To be on the Lookout' …… I am guessing she must have freaked out with Pastor Jim's 'warning' and filed a restraining order on me the next day.

I found out about all of that the following Sunday when Pastor Jim walked up to the front of the church and told me to pick up my Bible and leave his church service....I was more brokenhearted about that than anything that had ever occurred in my life up to that point.

…….. How could all of this have possibly happened!!???… I went to a new Church, …. and ended up with a restraining order against me from both Alicia,…. and the Church, that has a sign out front that says 'All Welcome.'

The last conversation I had with Alicia was only a couple weeks earlier after she got to work when she returned my phone call that she had missed earlier in the morning, just to say good morning and wish me a good day.

We had not had any argument or even any disagreement. There was always just all good feelings for me with our every conversation. ….. I thought about all of this over and over again repeatedly in my mind and finally said in my thoughts, *"How is it possible Lord that I could go to a new church, and end up with a restraining order against me???????"*

What Would We Do If We Knew?

I often painted a smile on my face to mask the sorrow I carried in my heart. Sometimes our sorrows show on our face and in our eyes, even to strangers. Sometimes only those close to us can see that something is wrong from our normal self.

Perhaps an act of kindness on our part, holding the door open for a stranger, or even a kind word and simple hello to a stranger in passing is all it takes to keep someone's heart from breaking completely in two. It costs us nothing to show kindness to all those we pass by and we may never know to whom we became the breath of air that they needed to experience, to survive.

What if? ….. We had the chance to do something all over again. To say something we wish we would have said to someone we loved, when we could have, or perhaps not to have said something we did say, that we later regretted.

What if? ….. We lived our lives with the subtle thought in the back of our minds, that tomorrow may not come for either ourselves, one of our family members, those closest to us and dear to our hearts or just one of our good friends.

What would be the most important thing to do or say if *ONLY WE* knew the future and that time was running out for ourselves, or another, *BUT,* we were *NOT* allowed to tell them and we had to keep the knowledge of it to ourselves and we were only allowed to take *ACTIONS* in the presence of that knowledge.

'Terminal' illnesses do have at least one bittersweet blessing. They foretell the future or the possibilities that the future holds, allowing us to take actions to do, or say something we may otherwise neglect. We have the chance to say goodbye and one more time "I love you."

Just as important we have the opportunity to spend time together with them, with that more than subtle thought in the back of our mind that there is, or at least may be, a time limit on us to do the things we want to do with them, taking nothing for granted.

Grandma Olga

In June of 1995 the last of my grandparents, my Maternal Grandmother Olga, passed away at 95 years of age.

One summer evening in August of 1992 I stopped by my Grandma's house on the way home from an errand to La Crosse that day. I had arrived about 6 pm to find Grandma standing in the front doorway of her home crying.

I immediately asked her, "What's wrong Grandma?" She told me that every evening she likes to go out on the front porch and sit in her chair and watch the kids and people go by and listen to the birds.

She said that she was getting old and was afraid to go outside anymore because it was getting harder for her to step up from the cement landing back into the house and she was afraid someday she may fall and not get back inside the house.

It took me less than a minute to come up with an idea and make a plan to help Grandma. I had just purchased some 4 x 8 sheets of plywood and a pile of 2x4's to build an office in the shop. I decided to take 1 sheet of plywood and build a platform out of the 2x4's to hold the sheet of plywood right up under the doors threshold, reducing the 8-10 inch step into the house to about 1 inch, which would enable Grandma to by herself, safely walk out onto her new little mini deck complete with safety railings, and this would now allow her to sit further out from the house broadening her view that had been restricted by the ornamental shrub trees.

That evening I helped her out onto the porch and back into the house again. I gave her a hug and a kiss and said, "I love you" as my last words to her that evening before I left.

The next morning I arrived early with a man to help me and a couple hours later the deck was completed.

I still remember the smile on Grandma's face as she thanked me. I gave her another hug and a kiss and decided the last thing I would always say before I went out the door was, "I love you."

As I pulled the door closed that day and my hand let go of the doorknob, I pondered in my heart which one of these visits might be my last visit, knowing that at 92 years of age the certainty of living becomes less and less with each passing year.

As I backed out of her driveway and I observed Grandma's new deck from the street, I thought that if she passed away the next day and only used her deck one evening and enjoyed her independence and dignity of self-sufficiency one more time, it was well worth any effort I had put into building it.

As it turned out Grandma lived nearly 3 more years in her own home with the help of a part-time house maid to assist her a few days each week.

I had the privilege of countless visits over those three years and with every parting, I never said goodbye, I instead, always gave her a hug, a kiss, and said "I love you" for my last parting words spoken to her.

With each of those visits, every time I pulled the door closed and my hand let go of the doorknob, the thought always crossed my mind, *might this be my last visit?* If it were, I knew that I had said and done everything I wanted to.

Grandma lived in her home all of those three years except for the last two weeks of her life. So my last visit with her was at the hospital, where she was still looking forward to going home again. I never did say goodbye to her, just when leaving her hospital room, a simple '*I love you.*'

When the day came that a phone call from my wife Meredith informed me of Grandma's somewhat unexpected passing, I shut the tractor off and just sat there in the middle of the field for a while after the call. I thought about the deck, the hugs, the kisses, and all the times I said "I Love You" instead of good bye. My hand letting go of the door knob so many times wondering when would be the last time, I now would wonder no more.

It was an unusual experience thinking about that she had finally passed on and there would be no more visits. I shed no tears, I had no ache in my heart at the news of her passing. I had no regrets,... I had... no .... regrets. I realized in a few moments why I had no tears, and no heartache, ... I had no regrets. I had said and done everything that was important between Grandma and me. Our relationship was full and complete in every aspect.

On the day of her funeral there were few tears shed, mostly stories and memories of Grandma's happiness in life and her radiant smile.

It was only when I stood alone by her casket thinking about all of the 'last time' visits I had with her and that my last words to her were, "I Love You," that I knew for sure my life and relationship to my Grandma was full and complete, void of any regrets.

I stood there by her casket a few moments more thinking little of anything, just looking at the familiar face that lay there before me, for the last time.

As I prepared my heart to leave and walk away from her casket, I whispered under my breath one more time, "*I Love You Grandma,*" for the last time. Only in that moment did my eyes fill with tears, because I knew it was, ... the last time.

Two Thoughts In Perspective

What if, we live lived with two thoughts regarding time, for both ourselves and others. The first thought is that we only have one more day together, today.... and the second perspective is that we will now live forever with no end to our happiness and plenty of time to do everything.

If we only had today all of us would likely call in sick at work and spend every moment with the one or the ones we love the most.

Wouldn't it be wonderful if we could have it all, hold both perspectives simultaneously, so that we can now enjoy every moment of our lives to the fullest.

As I made my way up the mountain the scenery was constantly changing as the altitude increased. The dense forest starts to thin out and you can see further and further through the trees and the sky starts to open up overhead. You start to experience the vastness of creation from a different point of view.

When I was walking in the dense thickness of the forest. I could not see the forest for the trees. As I started to break out of the forest at the tree line on the mountain, I could see the forest more clearly from above.

As I pondered these thoughts I wondered how that applied to my present situation. Was there something I wasn't seeing, something I was not understanding? Was there something good to come out of this, that I could not see or understand for the present?

As I searched desperately in my heart for answers, I thought back to the early 80's when I enjoyed excellent success in a planting and harvesting business for many other farmers and three years later circumstances from another situation I became part of led to me having to end up filing bankruptcy. I regrouped, downsized and went at it again with older and less costly equipment and then in 1990 took advantage of an opportunity to add a dairy farm to my business now having a better place to work from.

The cows milked well until the mid-nineties when stray voltage on the farm and some bad management decisions on my part eventually reduced my production by more than 75%.

This became the beginning of the end as bills started to go unpaid resulting in an avalanche of lawsuits and judgments against me. I was all but broke, and I probably should have filed bankruptcy again, but my pride wouldn't let me do so. Somehow I would have to figure out a way to recover and re-establish my business.

Ola And Martha

In October of 1996 I had the privilege to meet Ola and Martha, who were with a group of farmers on tour from Norway.

I had asked a lady crossing the street corner in Westby if she knew where the new Western boot store was at. She replied "I do not know, I am not from here. I am just visiting" in a heavy Norwegian accent. I replied "Er du fra Norge!!?" (Are you from Norway!!?) "Yaaaahh!!" was her wide-eyed expressive answer, quite surprised that an American was speaking to her in Norwegian. Excitedly I said to her, "Just en litt, Jeg må parke min bil, Jeg må snakke med deg!" (Just a little, I must park my car, I must talk with you!)

Martha, her husband Ola and her sister Liv were on a two-week tour here to take in the World Dairy Expo in Madison. I visited with Martha for some 10 to 20 min, together with Liv, who walked up and joined us a few minutes into the visit and we exchanged contact information.

Later that evening I drove to La Crosse to visit with other farmers in the tour group from Norway and then also met Ola. We hit it off good right away, had many things in common, and both of us liking John Deere tractors best.

Two weeks later I had the chance to buy a very cheap ticket to Norway and called to ask if I could come to visit and stay with them.

That was the beginning of my trips to Norway, always staying with Ola and Martha for free and helping them with whatever I could in appreciation for their hospitality.

We have visited each other back and forth over the years with each of us experiencing each other's country many times.

I knew the business failures I had experienced had opened the door to my opportunity to spend time in Norway.

As I walked here now among the sparsely spaced trees and shrubs just above the tree line on the mountain, the clearer view of the distant mountain tops and fjords reminded me to think about the bigger picture of my life.

My business failures had opened doors to new experiences. Instead of being tied down to the daily responsibilities of milking cows, I was free to spend time on the dream vacation of my life to my Great-Grandfather's homeland.

What I had dreamed about for many years of my life, to go to Norway and stand on the farmstead and land of my Great Grandfather Nils at least once in my life, maybe twice if I was lucky, would eventually become a reality and visits to Ola and Martha's farm became not just a once-in-a-lifetime trip, but what would turn out to be a new and regular part of my life.

With each trip I learned more and more words in Norwegian. My time in Norway and my desire to learn Norwegian as perfectly as I could, lead to the decision to buy a laptop computer in Norway that had all the extra Norwegian letters on the keyboard so I could practice writing in Norwegian.

Ola and Martha's oldest daughter Anita helped me to program my PC in Norwegian to force myself to learn more of the language. She also helped me to establish a Facebook page and I connected with many of my Norwegian friends, met many more and learned more of the language by reading the Norwegian Facebook posts.

I also established a 'Yahoo personals' account. I had fun learning to use my new computer while connecting with new friends from back in my home area in the States while I was in Norway. This gave us all something to start talking about as we became Yahoo pen pals.

Little did I know then that my Yahoo account would eventually connect me with the woman that would turn out to be the love of my life, Alicia.

A Quiet Place To Think

I stopped to rest on this area of the mountain for a while, where the view now extended across the fjords to the mountains on the other side, not that I really needed a rest because physically I was in great shape, the previous summer having actually ran up the entire trail on Vattefjell without stopping or even slowing to a walk.

I stopped just because I wanted to, to enjoy each area of the mountain path that held special memories of my walk that day together with Alicia, and Marc leading the way ahead of us like a pioneer explorer.

I sat down on the mountainside to ponder the thoughts and memories going through my mind about the time spent up here with Alicia and Marc later at the mountain cabin with all the laughter.

Joyful, uncontrollable laughter, lifting all three of us to a state of joyfulness and oneness, that for me elevated my emotions to a feeling of floating on air, experiencing everything in slow motion, fully enjoying 'The Moment.' Now savoring the experience of each of those moments that were now securely stored away in my memory.

As I sat there on the mountainside I looked out at Tingvollfjord to the East and Halsafjord to the North where Free Willy (from the movie of the same name) had somehow come to live after his release into the wild.

I thought about what it was that made Free Willy swim to Norway from the area near Iceland where he had been released.

What would have drawn him to Halsafjord to live, and to eventually die there? Why didn't he stay with the other whales? Was he rejected from the group? Was he searching for something? What was he searching for? Did he find it?

Did he find happiness and contentment in the attention he received from people there and those that would see him as he swam near the ferry boat as it crossed Halsafjord several times a day? or did even he as an animal, die of a broken heart?... alone.

Free Willy is buried in the Halsa area in a little park there near the shores of the fjord where he lived and died, with a grave marker to his memory.

From where I sat on the mountainside, I could see the land in Halsa near where he was buried. He had been living there and now he lives no more. He had swam in the salty seawater I was looking down at from my place on the side of the mountain, He would swim there no more.

He was swimming there in January of 2003 when my friend LaCinda and I came for a visit. Ola told me we could go there and probably see him swimming alongside the ferry, but we only had a short nine-day visit to Norway and Free Willy was not at the top of my list of things to do. I said we could go see him on my next visit to Norway... It never happened.

I was disappointed and a little regretful that I had failed to take advantage of a unique opportunity to visit a 'Movie Star' from a film that I had truly enjoyed.

Ola and I have driven past the road to the park many times and we have not yet stopped, but I am interested to stop one day to see what they have built to his memorial, because the movie about Free Willy touched a lot of people's hearts, including mine with an inspirational story of hope.

As I continued to look out over this land of mountains and fjords, with farms, homes, roads and communities nestled along and between them, I thought about sitting on the front porch of my Grandfather Julius's house on a Sunday afternoon when I was about 8 to 10 years old. I was listening to him and his youngest brother Selmer speaking Norwegian as they reminisced of stories told to them by my Great-Grandfather Nils.

I did not fully understand everything that they were saying in Norwegian, but what I could understand of the stories they talked about gave birth to my childhood dream to travel to Norway.

I distinctly remember making a decision sitting there that Sunday afternoon, that one day in my lifetime I would stand on the home farm of my Great Grandpa Nils, at least once in my life, maybe even twice if I was lucky...of which I have done.

I had made my two trips to Norway, and so much more. I have experienced winter, summer and every month of the year. The seasons of both planting and harvest, work time and free time. I have experienced some of the greatest joys and deepest sorrows of my heart here in the land of my roots.

I have shared also the joys......... and sorrows, of my friends here who have become like family to me in my heart.

Yes, I have experienced all that I had ever hoped for and more, a sense of complete and total contentment, having no need for anything more.

It is like a once-in-a-lifetime trip to your dream destination, be it Paris or Disney World. After experiencing the trip it would be nice to go back and experience it again, but the most important thing is that you have had the privilege to experience it at least once in your lifetime before you die.

My experience of knowing Alicia was like that. I had searched all my life for the something that I found every time I looked into Alicia's eyes.

I think I had dreamed about the Cinderella fairytale kind of love, for most of my life, and I have met many wonderful women and was married two different times to two of them, the first of whom is the Mother of my son Chris. They each were uniquely talented and the failure of my marriages was much more my fault than theirs.

The Woman At The Airport

Sometime after my second marriage ended, I met in passing in the hallway of the La Crosse Airport a tall beautiful woman in a long brown dress that was also wearing the saddest, empty look on her face that I had ever seen.

I said in my thoughts to the Lord as I walked *"Lord, how can a woman that beautiful not be happy?"*

As I looked upon her face, I noticed her eyes were looking down at the floor as she walked. About 20 feet away from me, she abruptly looked up and directly into my eyes as we walked toward each other, as if she had felt me looking at her.

We never broke our gaze into each other's eyes as we passed by each other only about 3 feet apart.

During those few moments in time I felt that I had looked into every corner of her heart and that instantly I knew her every hope, desire, fear, and joy; and likewise, I had revealed mine.

That was a day and a moment in time I would always remember. I thought she must have been a fashion model from Paris,…….. but what was she doing in La Crosse Wisconsin?

I would always remember her as *The Beautiful Woman in the Long Brown Dress*. Every time I thought of her I would pray for her in my thoughts and ask the Lord to care for her, whoever she was, wherever she was, and that she would have a good and happy life.

Most importantly, I prayed that the Lord would give her the understanding that I knew she needed to know, so that I could see her again one day in Heaven.

I did not realize it the day I met her in the airport hallway, but she would now come to mind with every single woman I would ever meet. It did not matter whether a woman was tall or short, slender or not so slender, beautiful or one that just blended into the crowd.

As soon as a new acquaintance caught my personal interest, I had to look them in the eye because I thought about the beautiful woman in the brown dress. I remembered the feeling in my heart looking into her eyes and I was searching diligently to find the feeling of that experience again.

Special Moments At The Amsterdam Airport

The funny thing was that from the moment I met Alicia in the church hallway, I never had a single thought of *The Beautiful Woman in the Long Brown Dress* until more than a year later in January of 2010, sitting alone at the Amsterdam Airport, with Alicia gone from my life.

I had a lengthy layover as usual between my flight from Minneapolis and my next flight to Oslo.

I actually always enjoyed the long hours between flights at this special and interesting airport. Although I have never toured the city of Amsterdam … yet,… I truly enjoyed getting lost in my thoughts as I roamed the Schiphol Airport, experiencing as much of the Dutch culture, food and atmosphere as I could absorb between each of my flights that routed me through this miniature glimpse of the Netherlands and the Dutch way of life.

The Amsterdam Airport would now also forever remain a special experience in my memory of February 28, 2009 when I returned back to Minneapolis on the same flight with Alicia after her visit to see me in Norway, when we searched together to find a special gift for Marc.

I knew where several shops were located throughout the airport and I led Alicia on her 'Treasure Hunt' searching for something unique that said *Amsterdam* on it that actually came from Amsterdam and not from Walmart or some other store.

Those same shops at the airport now hold the pleasant memories of that one afternoon when Alicia and I shared the experience together of shopping for something special for Marc with the excitement of two children on an Easter egg hunt.

Now, that particular day in January of 2010, I had exhausted the strength in my legs and arms from walking around with my carry-on luggage. I decided to rest for a while and I sat down next to two older ladies that looked well into their 70s'.

I struck up a conversation with them as I usually do with nearly everyone I come in contact with. I soon found out they were sisters, and that they were from Norway.

So for a few moments I forgot my lonesomeness for Alicia as I got caught up in a conversation in Norwegian with these two dear sweet ladies that reminded me so much of my own Grandmothers, Nora and Olga.

We only visited for about 15 minutes or so because they had to get going for their next flight on their vacation. We said our goodbyes and well wishes with the traditional Norwegian parting of 'Ha Det Bra'('ha day bra' have it good) or similar to saying 'Take care.'

As they walked away, I asked the Lord to care for them, and I thanked the Lord in my thoughts for allowing me to meet these two nice Norwegian ladies that had given me a much needed few moments rest from the heartache that I was carrying with Alicia's absence from my life.

The pleasant visit I had enjoyed with them was that breath of fresh air I needed in that moment to endure the lonesomeness of Alicia's absence.

As I sat there now alone again, my lonesomeness for Alicia came crashing back into my heart with a piercing level of pain, like salt rubbed into an open wound. The few moments of relief I had experienced from my heartache, made the heaviness of its return overwhelming.

I yearned for the sight of her smile and the tenderness of the look in her eyes..... I was sad to think that I would never be able to look into her eyes again.....and probably would never be able to find that experience again...... and then I said in my thoughts ... *"Wait a minute Lord!!..... I remember that feeling when I passed that woman at the airport in La Crosse!! ...and if it happened once with her, and again with Alicia... then there's Hope that it can happen a third time!!!"*

Then I thought, WOW!!!............... *I haven't had a single thought of the 'Woman in the brown dress' since the moment I met Alicia in the church hallway. .... "How can that be Lord, ? ... that I thought about, and prayed for a stranger that I had only met in passing, for years,.... and then that I have never had a single thought of her since the first moment I looked into Alicia's eyes in the Church hallway.......??"*

............For a few moments I was speechless in my thoughts,........... and then dozens of thoughts raced through my mind in a matter of seconds.

Did Alicia so completely fulfill what I had so briefly experienced years before?..............or is it *POSSible* that it was *actually Alicia that I had met in the La Crosse Airport that day!!???.......???*

Living Our Childhood Dreams

If it is possible, all of us want the fairytale love for our life. All of us start out in life with that kind of hope in our hearts.

Even as children we were read happy stories of hope and possibilities like Cinderella, Sleeping Beauty, and Snow White. I think most of us men want to kiss our 'Sleeping Beauty' and rescue her, or find our 'Cinderella' that fits the shoe we hold, and likely most women are hoping and waiting for their 'Prince Charming' to rescue them, and carry them away to live happily ever after.

It is that hope that each of us carry in our hearts that has become that single breath of fresh air that we have needed, to survive the heartaches that have beset each of us at times in the past.

It is that very hope that we can inject into the thoughts of the present moments, of the situations that come and go in our lives, never giving up on the dream of a 'Perfect Life and Love' ... Giving Hope, Life, and Love, one more chance.

The Mountain Cabin

As I continued up the mountain trail, I walked past Ola and Martha's cabin sitting on the top edge of the mountainside 100 meters or so to my left on my way to the top of the mountain.

I thought about the wonderful experience that day sitting in the cabin 'Stue' (STew-ah/a living room) with Alicia, Marc and I enjoying the beauty of Tingvollfjord in this mountain paradise, with all three of us laughing so hard together over a simple thing that we were exhausted from laughing.

What had happened was on the way back down the mountain we stopped at the cabin and made some coffee.

Sitting in the stue enjoying our coffee break, we each signed the cabin guest book, Marc, myself and then Alicia. As Alicia wrote, she said out loud what she was writing. She thanked Ola and Martha for their hospitality, and spoke each word as she wrote with a brief pause between saying each word.

As she wrote, she finished with thanking them "For..the..chance, ...For..the..chance, ... For..the..chance, ... to experience this."

All of a sudden Marc blurted out quite loudly, and laughing, "A CHANCE, of a CHANCE, of a CHANCE???!!!".......

Alicia and I looked at each other for a moment, and both of us burst out into uncontrollable laughter joining Marc! We all laughed until Alicia had tears in her eyes, and then Alicia said "It must be that the altitude is getting to me up here!!!" laughing so hard she snorted trying to catch her breath, and that sent all three of us over the top with hysterical laughter.

I remembered while we were laughing that shortly after Alicia and I met, I had promised her that the only tears I would ever bring to her eyes were tears of joy and happiness. I felt in that moment that I was fulfilling my promise.

I played that joyful memory over and over in my mind as I slowly meandered along my way to the top of the mountain.

I Just Needed To Learn To Listen

I then said to the Lord in my thoughts, ………. *"Lord,… I just don't understand………I JUst DOn't…U-N-D-e-rstand……………. I accept that Alicia is gone from my life, ….. but, I… just …don't… understand….."* …………… *"Lord you know that when I prayed about Alicia and I on the night of the fourth of January, about 10 pm,.. Lord …You KNow … that for the first, …and only time in my life up to that point,… I totally surrendered my will to your will, regarding Alicia and I, and our relationship to each other." "Lord, ….. if I was wrong about understanding your answer to that prayer regarding Alicia and I, … How can I have any confidence in any other perceived 'answer' to prayer from you????"*…… ……………………*??????*…………. and then I said out loud,….. "Lord,…….. I am not going to talk to you,… …..I am not going to pray to you,……………….. *Until you talk to me, and explain to me why I lost Alicia, ….. I am just going to shut up and listen."*

(do any of you men reading this, understand that most of us men *really do not 'listen?'* Often to the words that are spoken to us, and *more importantly*, the words that are not spoken, the *message that is spoken in between the lines?*…………)

It was very quiet in my mind the next day because I normally walk and talk to the Lord about anything and everything constantly in my thoughts as I work each day.

Sometime during the afternoon I was working quietly thinking only about memories of Alicia, her absence now from my life and tending to my work for the day.

Frustrated and exhausted from thinking about everything I thought, *"I want to do things for Alicia and she won't let me!!"*………… Then the Lord spoke to me in my thoughts and said, *"And I likewise want to do things for you, and YOU won't let me!!"*

…………The sound of the Lord's words in my mind had a distance and an echo to them, as if they were spoken in a large hall or auditorium.

The Lord's words jolted me, and I said out loud *"OK Lord, ……….you've got my attention,……"*

During the course of the rest of that afternoon, I had a half a dozen or so deep thoughts about my love and compassion for Alicia, and each time I had a thought about Alicia and my desire to do things for her, the Lord would give me a parallel thought about his love for me, and each person in the world and his desire to do things for both me and them.

With each of the Lord's thoughts to me concerning his parallel Love for everyone, I would later realize that this would be the beginning of my deeper understanding of *love, life and hope.*

I would begin to understand that perhaps the Lord allowed me to both fall in Love with Alicia, and experience the sadness of Alicia's absence and loss of communication with her out of my life, so that I could experience and better understand the message of His Love to all of us though the parallel of my feelings for Alicia.

Later that night as I lay down to go to sleep I could not remember all of the thoughts and understanding that I had been given that day, because each time I was given a new thought from the Lord, each new thought was so overwhelming that I could not remember the specific thought from a few seconds earlier when the new thought entered my mind…. Only the peace of mind and contentment that accompanied each of the day's thoughts remained in my heart.

It was a little easier to get to sleep that night after pondering everything that I could remember from any of the thoughts of the day.

I awoke the next morning well aware that I had slept a bit better than usual.….

Thoughts And Questions,…Write Them Down

As I was about to leave my room that morning, I paused for a moment and grabbed a sheet of paper and a pencil off from the desk and thought, *If I get anything else from the Lord today, I want to write it down right away so I can remember everything and think about it later.*

Sometime later during the day after having many thoughts about many things, I had the first thought that seemed especially important to write down on the paper that I was carrying in my pocket, and it was this, *God*

would not put me through so much suffering if he did not have a good purpose. ....
While I *believe* that,.......... I just do not understand it..................

Then many more thoughts began to come, one after the other..... *What about the funeral for Jeremy and Izzy.... If we believe in purpose..... What can possibly be any purpose in tragedies like that??* .... I feel that I am experiencing nearly the same sorrow and emptiness in my heart that Kristie must be feeling.

The most difficult thing to deal with is when you do not have a chance, there no longer exists a chance to say goodbye ...no possibility to experience one more hug and say goodbye. Only emptiness ....just air in front of you and that space never to be filled with their presence again in this life.

So many thoughts, they come and go so fast, replaced with the next thought and the previous thoughts are lost in the blink of an eye. I must write them down, the strong thoughts and lonesomeness....and the good thoughts, the good memories ... the inspiration. *Alicia, you are my inspiration.*

An event connected to an emotion is burned into my memory forever. All the thoughts in my heart, of my life with you a part of it, the moment our eyes first met in the hallway. The day-to-day events, the months, and the year together becoming a part of each other's life, all the big things, the little things and everything connected together, all passed before my eyes in my thoughts.

...Commitments I made to you and commitments I made to myself concerning you ...that I never told you. Commitments that I must now follow through with to be true to my love for you, and just as important to be true to myself, to keep my word to myself.

Promises easily made are sometimes easily broken. A 'Man of his word' is careful to give it, and once given, must faithfully follow through to the best of his ability.

.........I must follow through with my commitments to her, even if Alicia is not with me. It is only important that one day she knows that she was loved, and, is loved....

We are so quick to forget our thoughts..... write it down.

The Lord loves all of us enough, both believers and nonbelievers to give us blessings, even to those who reject him, and he still loves them as he lets them go their own way. I understand the fear of proclaiming love for Christ regardless of the consequences.

It is the same as proclaiming my love for Alicia. You are branded by some people who may misunderstand a pure and simple love of complete devotion, as an obsession.

When Jesus was on trial, he did not speak to defend himself even though he could have proven his innocence.

If he would have been on trial in a court of today, likely the judge would have ordered a psychological evaluation of Jesus.

Possibly the Psychologist would have come to the conclusion that Jesus had an 'Unhealthy, life threating obsession, with sacrificing his life for people that don't even know him, and people that dislike, despise and/or outright hate him.'

They could possibly conclude that since he loved all those people that hated him, … and they cannot understand why he would want to do that, likely 'He must be crazy or insane.'

Jesus was called a man of sorrows, and acquainted with grief. I can now understand that it was all day, every day for him. Jesus loved even Adolf….. more than I can understand that man's hatred for others.

Thinking about a verse in a song, … 'Come home, come home, you who are weary come home.'… It is a heavy sorrow the Father has for us that we may understand his love fully. It is his desire that we understand his heart. Not willing that any should perish and all come to understand what they need to know.

We are men of little faith….…. Abraham and Isaac, their faith….….. My faith in Alicia….…??? How can all of that fit together?…….. How does all of this exist? The farm fields, the fjords, the mountains, how does the earth hang in the middle of nothing, and yet stay perfectly in place, ….and Alicia is one third of the way around it, on this floating rock called Earth.

Driving the tractor back from Bøifot, to the home farm. …….. To see strangers walking along the way….….are they lonesome and empty? …or happy? ……

Apologize when you can,… the sooner the better.

Forgiveness…….… When you love someone….… When you truly love someone…….… they are forgiven even before anything happens.

If you 'KNEW' there would be no tomorrow… Would today be different towards those you care about? ….. or would you do more of the same?

If you could experience their presence again, or if they even were only present in a dream, your work day would be great, like the memory of having been out on a date, or a family celebration.

Their physical presence is not as important as the relationship status, everything would be okay, if there was JUST, communication....... A portion of perfect intimacy of the heart.

One or two hours a week of simple communication over the phone with one you truly love is better than all of the week filled with riches and pleasure that does not last.

Art & Marlene

As I worked in my office one day at a much later date than when the foundation of this book was written, I was making full sentences out of all the thoughts and incomplete sentences that I had jotted down in both English and Norwegian on the sheets of paper that I had carried in my pocket daily. As I read the preceding paragraph, I thought again about how happy I would be even now, if I could just talk with Alicia over the phone, for one or two hours a week, or at least 5 minutes a day several days of the week. .... I then thought of Art and Marlene .... and thought that I would add the story that follows.

I remember one day talking with Marlene, the widow of one of my dear friends who had been killed in a car accident a couple of years earlier. She said that the most difficult time for her was when Art was no longer there to call during the day or at least by 10:15 pm each night.

Her husband Art had devoted his life to preaching at gospel meetings that were often held in simple tents set up at various locations across the country for a couple, to several weeks at a time, depending on how many people continued to attend each night.

Art would call each day and return home each Friday night whenever possible between the weeks he was preaching to spend time with his family before leaving again for the Sunday night through Friday night meetings that he and another man would hold each night, meetings in which they had never passed an offering plate, and had never taken a single cent for their preaching. The Gift of God's salvation was free, and they preached for free.

They were able to do this because other Christians privately supported each of the men sufficiently to take care of their family expenses at home, and the local families welcomed them into their homes in the places where they were invited to preach.

It was these during the day, or end of the day phone visits that Marlene said fulfilled each weekday for her with Art's physical absence, as they both were committed to serving their Lord in this manner. She said that it was the silence of the phone at the end of the day from 10:00 to 10:15 pm that was the real evidence of the reality of his death.

Art's life of devotion to his Savior, his wife and family, as well as to the hundreds upon hundreds of people that had listened to him preach about God's message of Love and forgiveness in Jesus over the years, was solidly documented through the evidence of the large number of people that attended his funeral to pay their last respects.

A funeral which had to be held at the National Guard Armory to accommodate the more than 1200 people that came to the visitation, with over 700 people in attendance at the funeral, that had traveled from many places across the United States, and some from Canada as well.

Art's faithful service in preaching over the years had for many people, opened their eyes of understanding to the Love and Compassion that Jesus had for each of them.

A radio preacher from California once said, "Live your life doing something that will outlast it"

Art spoke at gospel meetings large and small, and likely the largest meeting he ever attended was that of his own funeral.

While the men that spoke at his funeral told the same message that Art had preached for so many years, likely it was the presence of Art's body lying in the casket, that silently spoke the loudest message to many of the people's hearts there that day.

Sitting among the crowd that day while I was looking at the casket, thinking about the still quiet body that lay there, I could still hear the sound and tone of Art's voice in my memory as I remembered both his preaching from the podium and personal conversations with him, as he so affectionately talked about his love and appreciation for his Savior, always expressing his passionate desire to tell others about the love and forgiveness in Jesus.

One of the sweetest sounds that I remember hearing in Art's voice over the years' was whenever Art spoke of his wife. Somewhere in a single sentence or in a longer conversation about his family, Art would draw in a breath of air, and softly exhaling he would affectionately say, "Ah yes, *My Marlene*"

The beautiful tone of affection that Art had in his voice for his wife of many years, was both a living, and ultimately a lasting testimony forever that the words of love that Art preached to others of the Love of Jesus, was actually displayed in both his public and personal life.

...... I can still hear the sound and tone of his voice even now, many years later.

...... I fully understand now with Alicia's absence from my life, how important those daily and nightly calls were for Marlene.

The Importance Of Communication

When I first went back to Norway after I had met Alicia, I called her every single day over the internet voice connection which cost only a penny or two a minute allowing us to visit for hours at a time whenever we wanted to.

I would wake up every night in Norway around 3-4 am which was 8-9 pm in Minnesota for Alicia so we could visit each night before she had to go to sleep, and then I went back to sleep for a while.

I also called Alicia every day at precisely 1:15 pm Norwegian time, which was the same moment Alicia's 6:15 am alarm was ringing. We always said Good Morning to each other with a 3-5 minute visit before Alicia had to start her day. I truly miss those phone visits with Alicia.

Once I have known her/you Lord, none other will do.... Faith is God's plan, it has to be that way. *'All things work together for good.'* No matter what comes I know that only Alicia fully satisfied my heart. All of the temptations are so present and I know that none of them can satisfy the emptiness I am experiencing in my heart right now. Only Alicia satisfied all of my heart for me.

Life Marches On With Or Without Us

This is another chapter of my life, but thoughts of now and then are one. Keep the focus, keep your eye on the prize when temptation comes.... Maybe one day.... Wait for that day. It will be worth the wait, just for the chance................ that we can be part of each other's lives again.

The old rugged cross is an emblem that speaks of God's love. ... What is my emblem, what am I known for? My love for my Son's Mother helped me to understand God's love for me. My love for Alicia has helped me to more fully understand God's love *and* provision for us,... No matter what.

My agenda is to win back Alicia's heart, ...if possible. Showing love in adversity is a more certain evidence of the purity of the love. Love without ceasing, pray without ceasing. She is altogether lovely to me, ... and it is written, 'He is altogether lovely.'

Before in my life I worked for myself, last summer, I worked to provide for Alicia and that was the most joyful for me now.

If I ever have the chance to be with her again, it does not matter where we are at, as long as she is there, whether we are poor or rich, or live in a little or a big house.

If my love is rejected, ... do I love still? And maybe I cannot marry her after some point of rejection, because I know that I am only human.

If I was not good enough before, why would I be now, or later? Do people marry for money, or for love?.............

"Holy Spirit draw nigh to me, love me, comfort me, be intimate with me that I desire nothing else....I need your comfort now...................................."

When I try to think, nothing comes,... put my paper away,....the new thoughts will come on their own. It has to be the Father's will.

Go For Broke

................Go for broke in love......................... There is a measure of fear in going for all or nothing. It does not matter if it is in a financial or a personal realm.

Many times gamblers use the term 'double or nothing.' ....In that term there is an 'equal opportunity' to gain as much as you stand to lose. ......It is simply a calculated risk that one may choose to take, or not take. That decision is usually made based on if that person can afford to lose the wager.

With some things we cannot afford to even consider 'Taking a chance.' Some people risk their very life to do a circus like stunt,... to prove what? That they have no fear?... and if they fail? ... what are the consequences?....

I was always aware of doing things safely in my younger years on the farm, never taking foolish chances in work or play.

God gave us a 'Good fear' in our subconscious mind to keep us alive. That 'good fear' keeps us from falling, from burning our hand on a hot stove, and throws our arm up to protect our head and eyes if something is thrown at us ...and because of my 'Fear of God'(a respect or reverence for God) that I acquired while I was growing up....I knew that I never wanted to take chances regarding things of eternity, which kept me always searching for an answer to my questions until the night of my 23ʳᵈ birthday when I found out what I both wanted and needed to know.

..............Sometimes I am just so fearful and afraid of losing Alicia, ... even though I have already lost her. ..... I was so certain about our future together, when we were together, that the thought never crossed my mind that I could lose her, until I lost her.

I must find a confidence in my hope to wait long enough to see if there is a chance, of a chance,... of a chance ....…......do not settle for second best, …..go for all or nothing, ...and......... be content with the outcome whichever way it goes.

Understanding Fear

I cannot be fearful of what the future may bring to pass in this life. Fears destroy people's lives by robbing them of the happiness that may be found in today, by worrying about what tomorrow may bring.

...I understand after Marshall's seminar that people are sometimes influenced by fears, *real*.... or only *imagined*, and that we all have at sometime in our life *reacted the same*, to *real* or only *imagined fears* and... we may not even have been aware of it.

The Power Of Our Mind

In July of 1974 I experienced something that I had *absolutely no explanation for* until more than 35 years later during his two day seminar in Vancouver the first weekend in March of 2010.

On that particular hot July summer evening in '74, I was driving to a sales meeting. I was wearing a white shirt and tie and had removed my suit jacket to be more comfortable as I traveled.

I had stopped and bought a cold can of Mountain Dew which I was sipping on as I drove with only my left hand.

All of a sudden my forehead started to itch badly and I needed to scratch it immediately! Since I was holding the can of pop with my right hand, I put my leg up against the steering wheel and let go of the wheel long enough to use my left hand to make one quick sweeping hard scratch across my forehead with all four fingers of my hand.

….. I had forgotten that I had received a long, large scrape to my forehead a couple of weeks or so earlier, and the hard fast scratch from my fingers ripped the entire 2 inch long scab from my injury.

The moment I saw the scab hanging on the end of my fingertips, I said, "Aaauughhhhhhh!!!!! …*WHAT did I DO that for*!!!!!... now my forehead is going to be *BLEEDING* when I have to speak tonight!"

Sure enough I could immediately feel the injured area start to get wet with blood after I had ripped off the scab.

At that same moment I was driving in somewhat heavy traffic maneuvering from one lane to another for my next turn. Since I was holding the soda with my right hand, I could do nothing about the blood that was now quickly accumulating on my forehead.

As I started making my turn at the intersection I felt the warm wet blood drop getting bigger and bigger until the warm drop of blood started to hang over onto the cool dry skin beneath the injured area.

As I was still negotiating the completion of my turn in the road, I felt what now seemed like an enormous drop of blood that had been hanging to my forehead, take off running down across my face. The blood drop ran across the inside edge of my left eyebrow tickling the hairs of the eyebrow landing on the left side of my nose, tickling also my left nostril, my upper lip and my chin as the blood drop scooted down across my face.

As all of this was happening, I quickly thrust my head forward to prevent the blood from falling onto my *white shirt*. A couple of moments later when the turn was completed I was able to divert my attention for a moment to look at the front of my shirt.

One glance brought relief as the blood drop had entirely missed my clean white shirt!

I found a place to set my can of soda and picked up one of the napkins that I had left on the seat from my stop at A&W the day before.

I now took the napkin and started to wipe the blood off from my face, starting with my chin, then working my way up to my lip, nose and eyebrow. I then held the napkin on my forehead over my injury for about the next 10 minutes or so as I drove.

When I thought that the bleeding may have stopped, I took the napkin away from my forehead and looked at it to see how bad the bleeding had been............. my first glance at the napkin that I held in my hand, left me *shocked and speechless. .... The napkin was still WHITE!!......?????*

I immediately looked into the rearview mirror and discovered that the reason for *no blood* on the napkin, was that the injury was *completely healed* and the scab was probably ready to fall off on its' own!

I immediately said out loud, "..**LORD**,......... I F-E-L-T *the blood drop* **run down** *my face!!!!!"*............. *"How could I have **p-o-s-s-i-b-l-y** have **F-E-L-T** an 'IMAGINARY blood drop' run down my face **tickling** my skin as it went!!????"*

I used to tell this story at sales meetings over the years as an example of the power of our minds. ...*BUT,* ... I only had '*Half of the story*'.

Understanding What Had Happened

It was Marshall's seminar in Vancouver that revealed to me, (as Paul Harvey used to say, *"The Rest of the Story"*,...(I loved Paul's program)) what had actually occurred that day with the blood drop running across my face.

He calls his seminar 'Turning Point' and that first Saturday morning was indeed a turning point in my *Thinking* and my *Life*.

The fears in our lives can paralyze us, *but only IF we allow them to do so.*

Our emotional reactions to fear, *real* or only *imagined*, each can produce the *EXACT* same physical reaction in our body. I learned that this is referred to as a 'Psycho-Neuro Duplication.'

I was so *absolutely certain*, and **Fearful** that my forehead was going to start bleeding, because I had the *'**Evidence that it would happen** from the **scab in my hand**,'......* that my mind produced the 'Psycho-Nero Duplication' *physical effect* in my body to '*Support my fears that ripping the scab off from my injury would cause it to immediately start bleeding!'*

This following example will help you better understand how this phenomenon can affect your life by '*experiencing it.*'

Likely every one of us has experienced tasting a *sour tart lemon wedge* that came with our glass of water and biting into it just to see how *sour it really tastes.* When you taste just a little bit of the *bitter, sour lemon juice* it now stimulates the taste buds on your tongue.

When you put the *entire sour lemon* wedge on your tongue you can now feel your tongue begin to tighten up from the *bitter tartness* of the *sour lemon.* When you bite into the juicy lemon wedge it squirts out all of the *sour lemon juice saturating your entire tongue,* and your tongue *now tightens up* from the *tartness* so much that it can even be difficult for you to speak.

Similar to the actual experience of the sour taste of a lemon, you can now experience the *same* or a *similar physical reaction* of the tightening of your tongue by *now* only *Thinking About* the sour taste as you watch a young child sucking on a *Sour Green Apple lollipop* as they make all kinds of funny faces reacting to their new experience of that *sour green apple taste!*

When we now understand this difference,… or should I say the **Lack of difference** between our *reactions to* **real** or **imagined** *taste,* and **real** or **imagined** fears, you are now able to realize that you can *choose* to control your emotions, by choosing to as much as possible *downplay* or *minimize your past fears,* and *Fully Focus On* embracing *Happy, Positive and Productive* thoughts.

The difference between you having a happy joyful life, (and often a more productive life) and those who are still striving to achieve those things in life, is mostly wrapped up *simply in the thinking you do every day,* all day long.

Fear, (or the *lack of fear with a confidence in ourselves,*) affects both the thinking and thus the actions or reactions of each and every one of us as individuals.

The better you are able to understand your fears, real or imagined, and how you react or respond to the emotions that were connected with those past fears helps you to better gain control of your present life and your future.

As A Man Thinketh

It is written, 'As a man thinketh in his heart so is he.'

….And it has been stated as well 'As a man thinketh so is he.'

These two statements are so very similar at the first glance, and yet so very different the more we think about the three extra words in the first statement, 'in his heart.'

In the first statement 'As a man thinketh in his heart so is he,' ... *'In his Heart'* adds the compassion, kindness and gentleness of us as a man or woman that has a 'Heart of Gold' personality to the outcome of our thinking, and *purpose of the heart.*

While both men and women can and do apply these good qualities of character to their thinking habits, not all people do.

Sadly, and often tragically, the bitterness, greediness, fear, hatred or revenge in some other people's heart's has affected their thinking as well, and the consequences of any of these negative attitudes in those people's hearts, when added to those people's thoughts has sometimes landed them in trouble with family, friends, society and/or the Law.

It is because of that, some of those people have sank to such a deep level of hatred and vengeful thinking that the actions of a few people in history have been referred to as 'Hard Hearted,' or 'Cold Hearted' committing crimes seemingly without any emotional attachment or completely filled with emotionally fueled hatred and revenge. ....The saddest thing to think about regarding many, and possibly all of these people is that most likely at one time in their lives they were someone's sweet innocent little child or grandchild, happy, smiling and kind.

What happened that they got on the 'wrong road' in life??.....

Likely it was because of a bad influence from a group of undesirable 'friends' or even a single individual, at school, work or social environments that may have changed the course of their life forever.

The statement 'As a man thinketh so is he,' could be referred to as simply logical, unemotional thinking.

The farthest to the one end of the 'emotional/unemotional' thinking scale that you could place this would be like the way a computer was first designed to 'think,' completely unemotional, not even logical.

The computer only made calculations, comparisons and assessments entirely based on how the computer was programed to 'think.' A graphic design program cannot do a profit/loss accounting statement or vice versa.

While the statement 'As a man thinketh so is he' seems to stand on its' own, it seems to me that it is difficult, maybe even impossible to remove the perspective of mankind's heart from the thinking process.

Even cold hearted or hardhearted is just a condition of the heart in thinking.

The Way Animals Think

Animals in the ladder of the food chain eat one another. Small fish are eaten by larger fish that are eaten by larger fish still, until you come to the whale, and man eats all of them.

Bugs, flies and mosquitos are eaten by birds, and mice and birds alike are eaten by cats and, larger birds sometimes eat all of them.

Any and all of these animals are killed and eaten by another animal with none of those animals having any regrets or remorse.

The Buffalo

I have been told that the Indians were sad and said a prayer of apology to the Great Spirit when they killed a Buffalo, realizing that they had to sacrifice the Buffalo's life so that they could live. The Buffalo provided dried meat to eat, their skins were used to make a covering on the tepee for shelter, moccasins to walk on and clothing for the cold winter weather. Their bones were used to make utensils and tools.

The Indians perspective of the value of the Buffalo's life to theirs' is such a beautiful picture of salvation to me, ...that Jesus had to die, so that I could live forever. The moment I understood this 34 years ago, God filled my heart with a perfect peace, and gave me peace of mind.

Love Moves Our Heart Into Action

I must give Alicia the peace she wants, in love. I willingly sacrifice my reputation for her, ...which only requires a small measure of my love for her. Sacrificing my reputation to protect Alicia's feelings because I Love her, is indeed a small, and easy thing for me to do, ... likewise, it leaves me speechless to ponder the enormity of God's greater Love for me, considering that He sacrificed *everything for me.*

Just thinking, ...Sometimes in life, we have to agree to disagree and just leave it at that.

I am at home and yet a stranger in this land, and I yearn for Alicia's presence. I can understand that my Lord Jesus yearned for the presence of the Father in prayer while he was physically here on earth. Like I yearn for restoration to Alicia, I only understand a small measure of how he yearns for restoration of each person back to himself,... it's far more than I can comprehend.

Am I embarrassed to speak of my life and my thoughts? He bore my shame,...for me. Can the thoughts and understanding given to me, be of a help to someone else??.....

My Two Dogs, Junior And Hoo-Hah

It is like the movie 'Pay it Forward.' ..... Love is all about him, and showing his love forward to others. .... This movie reminds me of my two dogs 'Junior' and 'Hoo-Hah' that I had on the farm.

Junior came with the farm from my cousin John, who got him from our Aunt Carolyn and Uncle Ron as a pup. He was a ½ Labrador, and ½ who knows. Hoo-Hah was a ½ German Shepard, ¼ Coyote and ¼ Hybrid Wolf pup that I got from Skip and Christine who worked with me.

Both Skip and Chris talked to each of their dogs as if they were humans and Chris taught her Coyote mix dog Kieta to respond back to her using sign language by touching Chris with her nose to her right or left, hand, arm, elbow, leg or knee for different things if she wanted to go outside, something to eat, drink, ice cream or a candy treat etc. Chris would say, "Smile Kieta" and she would show her teeth!

Hoo-Hah got his name because he was the first pup of Timber and Kieta's litter to climb out of the basket each day, and Skip would say "Hooooo-Hah, here comes that pup again!"

I would one day learn a fantastic insight of understanding into animals' behavior and thinking when Junior and Hoo-Hah came to the rescue and helped a neighbor's dog that became trapped after he broke loose from his dog house, dragging his chain until it got caught on some machinery parked out of sight up by the woods on my farm.

I thought it was odd that the dog food that I put out one morning was still there when I came home later in the day. The next day my neighbor Ralph stopped by and asked if I had seen his Rottweiler dog, and I said that both of mine had disappeared too.

Ralph said Sheila had driven all around the neighborhood searching road ditches and asking if anyone had seen anything. I had done the same.

After more than a week I had pretty much gave up looking for them. We began to wonder if someone was out stealing dogs.

Telling my story to a friend from town, Char asked if I would want to take her dog 'Harald,' since they were moving away and couldn't take him with them. So I took Harald home and thought that I would tie him up to the clothes line post for a few days so that he would learn that this was now home and *where the food is at.*

With his barking the first night, the next morning Junior showed up at the house, and then Hoo-Hah later in the day, …. I thought *'Uff-Da, now I have 3 dogs to feed.'* Then *Harald disappeared* the next day, and once more Junior and Hoo-Hah *disappeared again*! Now I really wondered what was going on.

I finally figured out later that day what was happening after my brother Craig and I went up by the woods to hook up a piece of machinery I needed to use. I drove back down across the field with the tractor and Craig drove his truck back alongside the field driving past some other things parked along the woods. When we got back to the buildings, he said "There's a dog up by the woods with a chain on him caught on some machinery." I said, "A small black and white dog?" thinking it was Harald. He said "No, A brown dog, A BIG brown dog" I immediately called Ralph and he said, "Yes, that sounds like its' Eli, I'll be right over." I told Ralph I would get some water and dog food ready and wait for him to give it to Eli, thinking he would be quite aggressive after more than a week without food and water. (I found out later that Char had decided to take Harald with her after all, and had simply stopped by and picked him up.)

When Ralph and I got up there Eli didn't even look at the food and only took a little drink of the water. There was rabbit fur a couple inches deep all around Eli, and yet not a single rabbit carcass in sight.

I realized in a moment that Junior and Hoo-Hah must have been feeding Eli rabbits they caught, then removing the leftover carcasses and had been staying with him to keep him company!!

Junior and Hoo-Hah had always hunted rabbits together, then laying face to face in the middle of the driveway they would take turns crawling forward to eat a few bites and then inching back a foot or so as each one of them watched while the other ate. They had now been sharing their food with Eli.

I was simply amazed at the wisdom and/or instinct, and compassion that God had put in these dogs' minds and hearts. They had the 'wisdom,'

or 'common sense?' to realize that Eli was helpless to help himself......
(I truly do not believe that there was that many dumb rabbits that would
have coincidentally run through a 5 foot diameter area so that Eli could
have caught them himself!)

It is something for us as humans to think about, the kindness that
Hoo-Hah and Junior showed to Eli in both *catching* the rabbits for Eli
to eat and then *removing* what was left over to keep the area clean of the
rotting remains, and finally just staying with Eli keeping him company
so he wouldn't feel lonesome or alone. (A good pet can be a wonderful
companion for us as well.)

It is amazing that animals can sometimes show more compassion of
the heart than human beings do. We can take a good lesson to heart from
the actions of these dogs. They 'volunteered' to help another in need. It
is good when we do the same. Acts of kindness always speak louder than
words regardless where the kindness comes from, be it a friend or a pet.

Certainties And Uncertainties

My work in Norway is like the Dugnad (volunteer work) we are not
the boss, a worker is like the messenger. We do the work of the master.
Do we talk about our belief in God or our love for our Savior. Do we help
others that we see in need. Am I afraid to proclaim to others my love and
commitment on a personal human to human perspective? Have we been
afraid to proclaim our spiritual beliefs to others?

Are we certain of those beliefs? I believe that some people that are
uncertain about their beliefs avoid talking about them, by saying that it is
a 'personal' thing with them.

I wonder what their first thoughts will be if they find out that they
were wrong and it is too late to change what they believe. Is it the same
now as it was for people back in Jesus' day on earth?

The pain of loss never leaves, you just learn to live with it,.... and from
it...... *"O Lord Jesus, O Lord Jesus, my heart falls into your hands to hold me,
how much you love me!"*

I must show faithfulness and love to Alicia, ...and to my Norwegian
friends, and all others back home. .... I have learned so much and, how
much more will I learn yet?

Maybe I haven't even begun to understand '*Everything*' of suffering and learning. Maybe one day I will also learn from the joy of Alicia's presence again.

As I was walking along the roadway from the farm I noticed that the new grass and weeds from this year are growing between the dead plants from last year. When last year's weeds and grass were alive, my joy was present as Alicia and I walked along them. And at the same time as the plants died last year, so my joy faded.

How long will I be in Norway? It doesn't matter, the day will come when I shall be going home, I shall be sitting on the plane. ....How long will I be suffering? I do not know the day, but I believe that it will come, the day that I shall be together again with Alicia, …….. Or at least that we can be the best of friends again.

Love, Life & Hope

And then the thoughts in spoken words came to my mind, *"And you shall write down all these thoughts of love, life, and hope in a book, ……………… ………………… And that shall be the name of the book."*

"WHat Lord,??!!......I'm writing a book???.... Write a *book*????.... on *Love,.. Life.. and Hope????* …………. okaaaaaay………………..…" *I must go back and add some more thoughts to some of the things I have already jotted down to better explain my thoughts ………….. and,……. I must write it from a Christian perspective…………. with a respect for other people's beliefs……* *because God doesn't force us to love him. ……. It is our choice.*

Value Outweighs The Cost

Ola and I were working on the floating stage at the boat dock. As Ola was tightening a bolt, a 19 mm socket fell off his ratchet into the sea water 3 to 4 m deep.

I told him I thought I could take a handheld magnet and fasten it to the end of a rope or a stick and recover the socket. He said that it would cost more than it was worth to retrieve it.

I thought *It's not about the money*, it was the challenge to me that was exciting. The cost meant nothing to me to do it on free time that we had nothing else to do, and I thought with some things, there is no cost too great. ....God spared nothing to redeem us. ... It does not matter how much it costs me, ...if it is possible, ...to restore my relationship to Alicia.

Him first.... Him first........ He is having his close time with me now. I have been experiencing intimacy of the heart with my Savior.

I think about my desire to be in Alicia's presence, and I understand more deeply his desire for restoration to each person. And I think, *How I shall treasure Alicia's presence again one day.*

It is easy to write a book, when you have something to say. The thoughts of your heart flow endlessly into words. Patience in love, hopes all things, believes all things, tolerates,...or rather I should say, endures all things, in love.

Looking out amidst all this beauty of the nature here in Norway, I feel empty,... that I have nothing in Alicia's absence.

I must proclaim my love for Alicia, with her or without her, to be true to myself. It is like Daniel and the Lion's den. He proclaimed his faith in God regardless of the consequences. In doing so he was faithful to both God, and himself, and what he stood for..... I have known some friends who are too angry in their heart to see the love in God's salvation.

I must tell many of my plans, to verify later that I followed through with my plans to set up some sort of provision available to Alicia whether she loves me or not. Love always, and like me waiting for Alicia, *the Lord is waiting for you.*

Tears Of Love, Compassion And Hope

This book is not written just to those who say they believe in God, it is written to the sad and lonely and those looking for hope regardless of what they believe. Look for the evidence of joy and brotherly love in people's actions, and not only in the words they speak. Anyone can speak grand words, but it is the actions of those words that have lasting value.

The beauty of a bouquet of flowers and the pleasant fragrance that accompanies it can touch the heart of the one who receives it. It speaks of the love and gentleness of the one who gave it. Tears of compassion sometimes grace the petals of those flowers.

I see the flowers of the field and forest as one of God's gifts to me to brighten my day and drops of the morning dew on those flower petals, like teardrops remind me of his compassion for me.

When you are filled with love, you do not see the wrinkles of age, the color of our skin, or anyone less than ourselves.

In the past, when I was angry, I forgave not. When I forgave, I was not angry. Forgiveness heals.

When you are filled with love it is not only about yourself, it is about unselfishly loving and respecting yourself and others the same........ Alicia, have faith in me to wait a little longer, I am who you thought I was.... For me it is all about Alicia, wonderfully all about Alicia.

In this book now, can I help others to understand what I am learning from both Alicia's presence and absence in my life?... Is it possible that I may write another book one day with Alicia back in my life?

There is nothing wrong with and most often nothing to lose to start over again to get it right the second time, or more if necessary. Right now it is like the song, 'On a hill far away.' It is too far away for me to see what the future holds.

The knowledge of how lucky and fortunate I am to have experienced both Love and loss of love personally and because of that to have experienced a greater knowledge and fuller understanding of God's greater Love for me, is a high that is higher than anything I have experienced up to this point in my life. Admit it or not we all seek some level of ecstasy in something....

Appreciate Both Pain And Pleasure

So quickly another note page in my pocket is finished, endless love produces endless thoughts.

Thoughts for the forward to this book........ To all men everywhere I seek to bring understanding and joy to your life both now and later. To men and women of all thoughts and beliefs I would that you find something important to yourself from my experience, as a parallel to your own life experience that you may discover a greater happiness in your own life. ....This is my perspective on *love, life and hope.* .....Show Love first whenever you can, because Life itself, gives us Hope. You may have an even better perspective than I. Because of my experiences I have better than I used to have. If we have a better perspective than some others do we can encourage them. I write this with a desire to help everyone understand better the giving of love and the love of giving.

Ask yourself, if you knew your life would be 'upside down' tomorrow, what would you do different today.

Today is the only day we have.

Live today with a perspective of love.

I also live today with the hope of looking forward to being together again with Alicia one day.

More is learned from pain than pleasure, and we can experience a deeper understanding in our lives by learning to embrace both.

The cold helps us to appreciate the warmth of the fire. Hunger gives us an appreciation for the food we eat. A starving man appreciates dry bread more than the rich man appreciates the meat he eats every night.

Listening

Monday the 28th......... It is early morning here, lying awake just thinking,... I wasn't listening and eventually she knew it.

She asked me one morning as we were driving to church, "What did I just say two sentences ago." I was able to repeat what she said, almost word for word to her. She said "Good I just wanted to see if you were listening." But I wasn't listening to what she was really saying between the lines.

For example; If you take the two words 'Drive' and 'Carefully', each word has it's own individual meaning in and of itself.

Each word can be used to describe several different and diverse subjects.

'Drive a car'/'Drive a truck'/'Drive a hard bargain'/'Take a Sunday afternoon drive'

'Fragile: Handle Carefully'/'Carefully remove the sliver from the eye'/'Carefully hand wash this garment.'

Combine the two words 'Drive Carefully' and most people will think about driving a car responsibly.

Now take a 16 year old that just got their driver's license and asks his older brother, "Can I borrow your car tonight?" he says, "Sure, Drive carefully." The next week he asks his parents "Can I borrow your car tonight?" They say, "Sure, Drive carefully."

Both his older brother and his parents responded to the EXACT same question with the EXACT same words, but each had an entirely *DIFFERENT* message.

The older brother's message was *'Don't SCRATCH it.'*

The parents message was *'We LOVE you and we want you back home SAFE.'*

I learned that the hard way another time here in Norway, as I later recalled in my thoughts and pondered Alicia's words to Marc and me that day, *"Don't go so CLOSE!"* while we were standing near the edge of a cliff by the famous Norwegian river Magalaupet, and I then finally understood the importance of what she was really saying,… …… *"I LOVE you both, and I don't want either of you to get HURT,… or WORSE"*…. that day between the lines.

She is still sleeping back home, and she is loved in my heart with the fondness that a mother loves a child.

The Links Between Mankind, The Nature And God

Intimacy between a man and a woman is the most beautiful gift God has given to us to experience. Children are the crown of that experience.

Some that know not the joy of personal intimacy, can find it in the joy of giving love to other people's children and any others in need, experiencing that oneness between two human beings by simply being the help and breath of air that they needed.

Spiritual intimacy is the most beautiful experience between God and man, and I personally believe that can be best understood in thankfulness within the saving grace of God, also in recognizing our partner in life as one of Gods greatest gifts to us in this life, as it is written, *'and the two shall become one'* as we find harmony in life with another person.

I believe that many people can find an enlightening measure of it,….. or a great portion of it in that spiritual intimate satisfaction in finding harmony with and in the nature in the presence of the creation and the Creator.

As One Dear Friend from Norway would tell me later *"Sometimes when I am in the mountains walking all alone in the midst of the nature it is such a beautiful experience of just being one with the nature that I just start to cry and I don't understand why."*

Also some people can experience this closeness to God when they are in the midst of trouble and cry out, *"God, if you are a God, help me."*

Alicia is my chosen one and I can still find a relationship with another if that time comes. God chose the Jews for Jesus to be a part of and they rejected him. He has given them blessings because of His love, and His same love is given to all others, including myself.

Once You Know, …You Can Never Go Back

Today I've been watching Frode painting the shed as I am hauling the silage bales in from the field to the storage lot. He never seems to be going very fast, but he is always making progress each time I pass by. You cannot un-paint what you have painted.

You can never go back to the unknown, once you know. I cannot go back to a state of unbelief once I have believed. I cannot go back to not knowing Alicia or forgetting about her, once I came to know her. I cannot go back to a state of unbelief in my Savior once he revealed himself to me so many years ago and I believed on him.

The thought of 70 weeks has crossed my mind, symbolic or what?? Deep thoughts…….. just a period of time??………. I believe perhaps that Alicia is just gone for a season. I just don't know how long that season is.

Faith is to believe that something will happen in the face of an absolute impossibility in the eyes of others.

I am easily offended because I am tenderhearted. It is good to be at peace waiting for God's plan and time to be revealed.

I can only guess at the joy that lay before me if and when we shall be restored to one another. I hold fast to the thought, appreciate and savor the moments of this hope.

I will never forget 'the famine time' of emptiness and loneliness….. What has he in store for us? Restoration of that which the 'locusts have eaten' of our personal time together?……. or something different for each of us individually?……..

….. I must write it down so I don't forget and can instead better remember my thoughts …… Unlike most women's ability to focus on many multiple things at once, most men can usually only hold one or sometimes a couple or so thoughts at a time.

As I walked here along the seaside of Karihavet, I think of what I have read, 'Come beside the still waters.' This is a place of refuge. The three small islands in the middle of Karihavet are symbols to me of refuge and safety.

What is security for Alicia? I could send her support each month as evidence of faithfulness, …..even if I were with another.

…If we donate money to different organizations and charitable causes, it would be just as appropriate to donate some form of support to someone we love, even if we are no longer with them. I do not only tell you my Love, I will show it.

Maybe,…. one day we will have the privilege to share beginning again, and enjoy 'just in our presence' in a new aspect.

Am I ashamed to write about my life?... He bore my shame for me….. Am I able to draw men and women's hearts to understand my love for Alicia?,… and help them likewise, understand your love for them Lord?

I am in the midst of a paradise here as I walk, and still I am lonesome without the object of my heart's desire, Alicia………. And so I understand much better now how much the Lord yearned to draw all men to himself.

We Gain Understanding And Wisdom From Our Experiences

Tuesday the 29th of June, …..Another day,… I kept believing everything was all right. *We learn from* our biggest failures and even *our small mistakes, or we are doomed to repeat them.*

Be thankful for the freedoms we have. Be bold to proclaim your beliefs, whatever they are,…. For it is who you are.

I had one dream of Alicia Sunday night. I remember and I am enjoying the memory of the beautiful pleasure of her presence. This morning I am a little disappointed that I did not dream of her again.

Learn to appreciate what you have, enjoy the good of the one dream. It is not so many months ago since we last talked, and the dream bridges the gap until the day I can talk with her again.

…..It is like that breath of fresh air to a drowning man.

It is like the song by The Carpenters, 'We've Only Just Begun'. All songs become ours, not just some to one and not another. Pleasant songs from years ago have now become special to me of Alicia.

I'm just lonesome today, not bad, just lonesome. Thinking about Kristie, and Jeremy, I must pray for her, as it is written, *'That we may comfort others even as we are comforted'*.... And also Lord, Al from Yonkers mission in New York who was on their Facebook post..... Al, others at Yonkers, Kristie, Kristie and Jeremy's parents .... So many others..... It's not just about me.

Well-meaning words carry little impact without the experience of what someone has gone through or is going through to back it up.

Sometimes we, myself included have said to someone going through a difficult situation 'I know how you feel' attempting to make them feel better. But often, unless we have experienced the exact same or a very similar situation we truly don't understand fully what they may be experiencing at the moment.

A recovered alcoholic can truly identify with an alcoholic or a person with a drug addiction that wants to change their life for the better.

A counselor who herself has been a victim of rape may be the only one that can truly both sympathize *and* empathize with a young woman whom has had that happen to her.

That counselor may have been a total stranger to the young woman, and in a moment of time in telling her that *she* has gone through the exact same tragic experience, and *understands* how she is feeling, can be a greater comfort to the young woman than all of her family and friends, regardless of how much her family may all deeply love each other.

Hope

Hope, *Never* give up hope….. *Never*….. No one can take it away from you, unless you let them.

Love

Love…. it is from love that we learn about life. Without love for *someone or something* in life, do we really have a life? Without love, we are left in despair, and lack of purpose in life.

I wonder what kind of husband I would be to Alicia now, better than I would have been before? ….I wonder what kind of husband would Alicia say I would be now compared to what she would've said I would have been before?.........

I have so many thoughts and questions, ... There has to be something to go with all of this.

He shall supply all my needs and more. He shall be my contentment......
I find it in him and also what I do, and not do concerning Alicia.....
Waiting on the promises of God..... If I asked my Father for bread, will he give me a stone?... Drawn to and compelled in life and hope, ...

I have missing thoughts here, so many came I could not write them all down before I forgot some of them.

What was forgotten can be remembered when the time is right to receive it..... The Lord has remembered us in salvation.

Forgotten thoughts,......? What are they?........ It is only just important to wait for the plan of the Lord to happen.

I am a long way from home, and 5000 miles or 1 mile, I'm still not there, mentally or physically, ...it seems it would make no difference.

The day of my wedding shall be one of the most wonderful days of my life, ... If I shall have another wedding day, will it be with Alicia? or someone else? I will share that joy with others.

The day of my salvation was the same for me, and I have shared that with others also as the opportunity to do so has allowed.

Understanding Our Experiences Is The Beginning Of Wisdom

.... I believe that I shall receive many more thoughts, of Love, Life and Hope. ..... I am beginning to understand more and more.

It will be worth the wait for Alicia, ... not just for the certainty that she will be there one day,.... It is worth the wait, ... for the Chance, of a Chance, of a Chance, that we can be a part of each other's future.

My whole life and purpose from my perspective now is built around her needs and wants, if she will one day allow me to do things for her. I understand now how the Lord feels and does the same thing for our provision. .... Take a chance now, or live to regret that you didn't.

Facebook Post: Many paths to God? .... No, I believe only many paths to the cross, which is the door to God. ....I am thankful to the Holy Spirit for all the desires of our hearts, to be used for good to ourselves and others.

There is a song playing on the radio that I remember was playing on the ferry boat when Alicia and Marc were with.

The song now seems empty without Alicia here. The emptiness that accompanies the absence of Alicia and Marc, burns the experience of it into my heart in such a way that if I have just one chance to be together with Alicia again, the memory of her absence will guarantee that there is not a single chance of failure.

I believe if we have the privilege to be together again, our joyfulness will exist as a solid rock, steadfast and secure. The three strong islands in the middle of Karihavet speak to my heart of the Trinity, silently and steadfastly standing in the middle of a place of refuge.

A Song on the radio is singing, 'Guilty feet have got no rhythm'..... It is like going through the motions of life without a complete purpose...........

..............*Am I embarrassed to write and tell about my feelings for my friends and neighbors to read??*................

Thoughts like these controls our behavior directly and indirectly for each of us........... and then the Lord spoke to me in my thoughts, *"Write what I tell you or you won't get anymore"*.............. and with that thought from the Lord, I realized that it is important to me, that as many people as possible, should have the opportunity to benefit from my experiences.

Waiting, waiting, waiting. Nothing is coming in my thoughts right now, just waiting for what comes next. ..... In the meantime I must do what I can, that is important, for myself or others that shall last beyond the present moment.

Words And Actions

(Postcard) *My Dear Beloved Brother, Pastor Jim. You have warmed my heart today because of your respectful reply. I had my Mom open and read my mail to me over the phone, and then she forwarded your letter to me here in Norway and I will take care of it from here. It meant a lot to me that you signed your letter, 'Respectfully, Pastor Jim'.... Respectfully, Curt*

.....How I yearn for Alicia's presence. How the Lord Jesus yearned for the Father's presence in prayer. After the testing comes joy, extraordinary joy and the joy is always in seeing the completion of his will, and it is always for our good.

…..Regardless of the outcome in this life, of a certainty Alicia and I shall be restored to our friendship again in Heaven. I look forward to that day even as we look forward to seeing our Savior.

I can now understand how the Bible was written, as I receive thoughts of comfort and insight from the Lord.

In my conversation with those who do not believe as I believe, it is my purpose to faithfully tell them what I believe when they ask me, and when given the opportunity to do so, to show them by my actions and encourage them in all things in this life, that they may desire to know more of what I believe.

It is sad to see some people preaching religious words of God's love and not showing it in practice…. Why would anyone want to become like them.

Those people simply lose ground with the person they are speaking to, and push them farther away from understanding God's genuine Love.

It would be more profitable to show a simple kindness to them…. Actions speak louder than words.

I have told most everyone I talk to about Alicia, and I have told some people that I have a plan to provide for her in the future even if I am not with her.

Some women I spoke with didn't like that and said that I should not give her anything…. Some thought it was very nice of me to do so…. And I discovered with those statements that it was very easy to determine if that woman had a selfish, or…..a kind and generous heart.

God provides for us even if we do not obey and love him, because he loves us. He also promises and provides us more good things if we do obey. It is an example of God's love for me to provide good things for Alicia, and also to others as well.

I remember the day that the cabin was filled with the joyful laughter of Alicia, Marc and I.

All of the beauty in this land is nothing to me if Alicia is not in the picture, just as all the riches in the world are nothing to me without Christ.

…… Thinking about Job, his friends railed upon him, Judged him, and yet God blessed him.

Pastor Jim's letter in a spirit of cooperation meant a lot to me. I look forward to his embrace and restored fellowship. Only the Lord can resurrect the dead for us. It is he that will restore us to the place we were and that day shall be perfect in him now.

Powerful Words And Experiences

To be truly happy in this life, we need three things. We need something or someone to live for, something or someone we are willing to die for, and something to hope for.

July 1. I had a dream of Alicia last night. We were at a meeting and she came over and touched me on the shoulder. I touched her back on her shoulder and then I took her in my embrace. It was a powerful experience.

The power of words, ...What is one or two words that are so powerful that they say it all. Pastor Jim signed his letter to me *'Respectfully,'* and that meant more to me than I can put into words.

I think of the story I read about H.G. Spafford, a prominent and successful lawyer from Chicago, who lost all of his Real Estate property in the Great Chicago fire. He had also lost his 4 year old only son to scarlet fever. He later decided that his family needed a vacation and chose to go to England where his friend D.L. Moody would be preaching. He sent his wife and four daughters ahead when he was delayed by business. He received a telegram from his wife after they were shipwrecked and she arrived in Paris. *'Saved Alone, What shall I do?'*

He immediately booked passage on the next ship to be with his wife. He asked the Captain to notify him when they were passing over the spot where his daughters drowned. En route the Captain came to his room and told him *"We are about over the spot right now."*

As Horatio Spafford looked upon the watery grave of his children, he penned the words to the song, *'It Is Well With My Soul'* ('When peace like a river, attendeth my way, When sorrows like sea billows roll, Whatever my lot, Thou has taught me to say, It is well, It is well with my soul.')

The power of words, simple and bold, that encompass the joys and sorrows of our hearts and experiences. They proclaim who we are, what we are, and most importantly what we stand for.

With seemingly all that had happened with Pastor Jim, his simple use of the word 'respectfully,' humbled me. A multimillion dollar amount would likely have not brought as much joy to my heart as his simple use of that word regarding me.

What effects do the words we use, have on others? .... To the glory, or shame of our Lord.

AAAHHHHHH!

One day when I was custom harvesting corn silage for a farmer, I drove into the farmyard that morning and parked off the side of the driveway. He was standing next to his truck and trailer and asked me if I would help him lift the loading ramp plate up.

As we lifted it up I did not see that I had all eight of my fingers in the support stand hinge and pinched all of them very badly. As I let out a very loud "AAAAAAAAHHHHHH !!!!," He said "I am *SORRY* I forgot to tell you to keep your fingers back.... Man, that's *REally* got to hurt." ......I did breathing exercises for 2 or 3 minutes like I was at a Lamaze class.

Later that same day I broke an electric clutch wire on the forage harvester, and the farmer came down to the field where I was repairing it.

As I was using a jackknife to prepare the inch-long wire to replace a connector, I somehow pulled the whole wire off leaving less than 1/4 inch remaining. I said "AAAAAAAAHHHHHH, what did I DO that for! I'm so angry at myself!! How could I be so STupid to break that wire off!!!!!!.....AAAGGHHHH!!!!".........

The farmer said to me, "Man, don't you *EVer* swear??" I just humbly said silently in my thoughts, *"Thank you Lord for bridling my tongue"*.

For more than 30 years that farmer and I had been discussing our beliefs and faith. That day I said more by saying nothing, than I had said in 30 years of talking.

The Old Homeless Man

Our choice of words can have a profound effect upon those whose ears they fall, even if we do not know them.

At a church conference in Chicago about 25 years ago, I was sitting behind two young women on the bus who had been missionaries and they were talking of their experiences. They were talking about what they had to give up in their life for that job.

As I followed them off from the bus one of them boastfully said to the other, "We're talking sacrifice here!" as we passed an old homeless man standing on the street.

As I passed by the old man walking immediately behind them, I heard him sarcastically mutter under his breath, *"S-a-c-r-i-f-i-c-e!!"*..... "Humph!"

All I could do for him was to pray that someone would show him a measure of kindness. I have never forgotten that old man, and the emptiness that must've existed in the final years of his life.

A Clear Perspective

Sunglasses shift the color and hue of life that we may see it more clearly. I always keep them in one place in the car so that I can always find them the moment I need them. Seeing life through the love of God's eyes also helps me to see life more clearly, ...and he is always right there the moment I need him.

Something always reminds me of something, or someone, and it seems that nearly everything reminds me of Alicia.

I am happy today because of *hope*. Pastor Jim's use of the single word *respectfully* has given me hope that at least he will not discourage Alicia regarding me... And possibly encourage her one day.

I'm having one of the best days I can remember for a long time. I have a glimmer of hope. That is everything right now for me.......

Kristie, what is her present hope? ... What would it be for her to see and hold Jeremy and Izzy, even one more time if that were possible............ I'm not sure if I could handle what she must be going through.

A Courtroom Blessing Of Understanding

I must be open to God's direction and thoughts when they come.

I thought back to sitting in a court room listening to the court read Alicia's accusations against me. I still do not understand it, or what went wrong, but no matter how bad it seems, for the one you Love, you will lay down your reputation, or your life.

While I was listening to the accusations I thought about what I would have to say to defend my reputation and realized that I would have to disgrace Alicia's reputation to defend mine.

Thoughts of Joseph and Mary came to mind. When Joseph found out that Mary was expecting a child, he naturally believed that Mary had been unfaithful to him and resolved to 'divorce' her.

As I understand the custom of the day, if a man's betrothed 'Wife' (We say 'Engaged' now) was found to be unfaithful before they came together as a husband and wife, the man could bring his betrothed 'wife' into the public square of the town and publicly proclaim the unfaithfulness, disgrace the woman and defend his own honor and officially 'divorce' her.

It is written that *'Joseph, being a just man resolved to put her away privately,* (divorce her privately) *not willing to make her a public example.'*

In that *MOMENT,* sitting there in the court room, I realized the great and compassionate Love that Joseph had for Mary........ *'Not willing to make her a public example'.*...... He wanted to protect her feelings, ... regardless of any embarrassment to himself.

I looked over at Alicia sitting at the table across from me, and I could only feel more and more Love and Compassion for her until my heart was filled to overflowing with *joyfulness* that I had the privilege to know and fall in Love with Alicia.

......If you need to, you just double the love you put into it. Enjoy the good moments, and it helps you to endure the sad ones.

The Little Dog That Saved My Day

Enjoy the moments. I remember a moment almost 30 years ago one February afternoon. I was very heavy hearted about the situation I was in.

The sun was shining brightly one day after we had a large snow storm a few days before. Even though it was the most beautiful day we had for a while, I was still heavy hearted as I drove through the streets in La Crosse.

The snow was piled high between the streets and sidewalks, and as I was driving I noticed a little dog running on the sidewalk to my right. I would see him each time he passed over a driveway between the snow banks. I was simply observing him running alongside me at the same speed.

All of a sudden while he was running on the ice and snow, he came to a driveway that was completely clean. He must've been trying to stop, and when his feet hit dry pavement, he tumbled end over end, and stood up in the driveway looking like *'What just happened to me?'*

I laughed so hard that I forgot my sorrows for a moment, and as I realized that I said out loud, "Thank you Lord for the laugh! *I needed that*!"

Learn to appreciate the joyful moments in between the times that are not as joyful, and remember when you are experiencing some sad moments, there will be more joyful moments to come.

Purpose in your heart to enjoy the good moments and good days whether you are alone, with someone, a special someone, ... or your most special someone.

Allow no one to steal your joyfulness from you, not even the devil himself ..... especially not him. Choose to be happy.

Experiencing Satori For A Contented Life

I am hauling round bales off the field today at Skjelvåg. I have been observing the contented life of the beef cows on pasture. Each time I return with the tractor to get more bales, some of the cows have meandered further across their pasture. Some are lying contented in the sunshine just chewing their cud. It seems as if they have not a care in the world and that probably is so.

They are just enjoying the moments of their life thinking neither of yesterday or tomorrow.

Most of us have observed both outdoor cats and house cats living their lives in the same manner. They live in the present moment, the *'Here and Now Moment'* sometimes best described for me by the word *'Satori'*.

Satori is a Japanese word for *'comprehension, awakening or understanding.'* I was taught that Satori also was used as an expression of perfect awareness or perfect contentment in the present moment. I have come to appreciate the thought of a state of *'Perfect Contentment in The Moment.'*

It is OUR choice in life, for example, that some people choose to smoke and some people choose not to smoke.

I was told a story about a man from my home area of Wisconsin that picked up a man hitchhiking on a cold January morning. The man was very glad to get out of the sub-zero cold and into a nice warm truck.

The driver of the truck was smoking a pipe and soon after the hitchhiker started to get warmed up he abruptly told the driver "You know,... if God would have wanted you to smoke he would have put a chimney on you!"

The truck driver immediately slammed on the brakes and came to a stop. He told the hitchhiker "Get out!" The hitchhiker said, "I thought you were going to give me a ride?" The driver answered him, "If God would have wanted you to ride, *He would have put wheels on you!*"

We have no right to tell someone else they cannot, or should not smoke, UNLESS, they are OUR children, and they are under the age of 18. After that, it becomes THIER choice. We can voice our concerns to the ones we love for their health, etc. ..... ANd we must respect their choices, even as we expect others to respect our choices.

I have come to understand that people smoke for example, to achieve Satori. It brings them into the present moment of contentment..... (People tend to overeat their favorite tasty foods for EXACTLY the same reason......) In the present moment, the '*Here and Now Moment*', we can be NEITHER, depressed OR anxious and stressed out.

Sadness or Depression is a result of '*thinking*' about something that has ALREADY happened in the past that we either regret DOING, or regret NOT doing.

Nervousness or Anxiety, and the stress that goes along with it is a result of *worrying* ('thinking') about, or fearing something in the future, that has NOT YET happened, and/or may *NEVER* happen.

Smoking, drinking, or eating, (anything touching the tongue *stimulating taste*) brings us into the 'present' or '*the here and now moment*' helping us to '*escape*' the 'past depressing memories' or the 'future fearful worries' for a little while, ...for as long as the cigarette lasts, as long as the bottle of beer lasts or as long as the bowl of strawberries and ice cream lasts.

Music, a hug, a back or foot massage, the warm sunshine upon us lying on the beach, etc. ... each likewise stimulate a physical pleasure helping us to *escape* depression *or* anxiety into the *present moment*.

Understanding these emotions fully, and the reasons for our reactions to each of these things, helps us to achieve *a happy balanced life* by choosing the 'right things' to stimulate the 'right reactions' to achieve a happy state of 'Satori'.

I am very content today, content, very content. Perhaps for this moment today, I have taken a lesson from the cows and cats..... I'm still aware of yesterday, and the past, and I can think about the future, but I am truly focused on today and the pleasantness this day holds..... The cows and cats live in a wonderful world.

Thank you Father for all you've given me. Something to eat and drink, be it bread and water, or steak and cake. And you have given me love, of yourself in your Son, the best you could give. And to teach me about Love, you gave me Alicia. Thank you for allowing Alicia to be a part of my life. I have experienced perfect contentment. Just Alicia, nothing more, nothing less, just Alicia. Alicia is everything to me right now. Amen

If you've never truly experienced being *'In Love'*, I can understand that you do not understand this. If you have *experienced* a genuine love, then you do understand what I am saying.

If you do not know Jesus, like I know him, I understand that it may be a challenge for you to try and understand why I appreciate him so much.

You can now easily better understand that I truly appreciate Alicia, and that I gladly did whatever I could for her on her behalf.

So many years ago now, God used my understanding of my love for my son and my son's mother to reveal to me even more, how much Jesus loves and cares about me, and that helped me to finally understand why he took my place on my behalf. If you do know him the way I know him, then you do fully understand my *appreciation* for him.

If you are now seeking to more deeply understand the depth of God's love for us, you will gain a deeper appreciation for him as you learn more and more about him. When you understand how and why so many people appreciate his love, because of what Jesus did for us, you will also now know him.

Instant Friendship

I had a friend that asked me what I was going to do one evening when I said I was driving to a certain town.

I said I was invited to a certain man and his wife's house for coffee. He asked why.

I said "They are good friends of mine." Bewildered he asked me how I could be good friends with them since he knew that I had only met them one time in a business situation.

I said we instantly became good friends the day we met. Still bewildered, he asked "How can that be, you only talked with them for about half an hour."

I explained to him that we both understood the same thing about Jesus, and each of us knew within a few sentences, that each of us understood what the other one understood about him that was important. We knew, that each of us knew, that we knew what we needed to know!

An example that can help you better understand this is, suppose that you and I each have a message for one another in a situation of war.

The safety of many depends upon each you and I, giving our message to the correct person. We have a code word to be used in conversation between us. And we each have two more follow-up code words to be used in conversation that give each of us absolute certainty and confidence that we can trust one another. We know, that we know, that we know!

It is like that when people tell you what they believe or don't believe. Sometimes it is obvious that we do not believe the same thing about a belief in God or not, or just a about a social issue or a principle.

Initially we can think we are on the same page with someone, but it is the continued conversation that gets us to the certainty of common ground or that we hold the same or different beliefs or positions on something.

Respect, Reconciliation

July 1, 12:30 PM Respect, ...the most important thing is to not have disrespect. To empty yourself of bitter feelings, if you have any, and to hold everyone in the highest respect you are able to give them.

The joy of reconciliation, we all always look forward to it. I look forward to it. I'm thankful for it......... I'm thankful to Pastor Jim for it as he confronted my heart with it that first Sunday morning I went to his church, …………….. And he doesn't even know what he did for me, and yet I am thankful for it………. Seven years of bitterness were gone in a moment.

I had refused to speak to two certain people (who both professed to be Christians) for over seven years. They had said something about me that was untrue. Not only was it untrue, …. It was the EXact opposite of the truth. I found out later that they had been told wrongly by a man, and they were just repeating what they were told.

That is the seed and poison of gossip.......I wonder how many times in my life I have been guilty of the same?? ...I knew it was wrong to hold the bitterness against them, but I still held on to it anyway. I used to think that when each of us got to heaven the bitterness would be gone and we would be restored in our friendship.

I am not sure exactly what happened or how it happened, But when I decided to go to the new little community Bible Church that seemed to stand out from all the others in the phone book, I simply felt that the Lord wanted me to go and offer to sing a song for the church service, and it brought me to Pastor Jim's service.

I have often been invited to sing for different church services or special meetings and I always have taken every opportunity to do so.

I went an hour early to have an opportunity to talk to the Pastor and when I offered to sing a song for the service, Pastor Jim said "Not until you've been here for six months you won't." ...... Immediately I thought 'He's using discretion, and is *testing me* to see if what I believe is consistent over time.'

My respect for his comment probably influenced my reaction to his words later in the service, just before communion.

When the time came at the end of the service for what is called breaking of bread, Pastor Jim said "All are welcome to participate, but let each man *examine his own heart*, and if anyone has anything against a brother, let him first go and be reconciled to his brother and then come back to the Lord's table"

Immediately my certain two friends came to mind, and Pastor Jim's words cut deeply into my heart. I knew I needed to go and forgive them, even if they did not apologize to me..... I said to the Lord in my thoughts, *"Lord, I am going to participate in the breaking of bread today and before I come back to next Sunday's service, I will go to talk with them and forgive them."*

I had now made a commitment and I had to follow through with it no matter what before I came back to next Sunday's service. It took me until Thursday morning, and then I went and made the visit to their home and told them I forgave them for what they had said. We had a nice long visit over coffee with the restoration of our friendship. Having fulfilled my commitment to the Lord, I could now go back to Pastor Jim's service with a clear conscience.

The Schoolhouse

Shut off the radio, and 'pause'(the Norwegian word for pause, spelled the same and said 'pow,sa'),.... To think........ Is everything lost with Alicia? Will I be able to talk with her one day? Will I be able to show my love to her again one day? ....

So many thoughts ...... I am driving by Ola's three vacation houses right now. Ola and I walked through and looked at these three houses some years ago before he remodeled them. He explained everything he planned to do to make the houses nice.

Back then I did not he see his vision, I just thought they were old houses and an old one room school building.

It never crossed my mind back then that one day I would enjoy being here at the wonderful schoolhouse with Marc and Alicia, and only a year later everything would be lost. It seems as if I can recall every moment the three of us spent here. ....Precious memories.

At least I've been sleeping better after I found out that Pastor Jim signed his letter *'Respectfully.'*

Beliefs, Words, Actions

Thinking about what I have learned from Marshall's seminars, is all this coincidence??.... or purpose?............. I do not think it is coincidence .... it has to be purpose, and maybe just a long test.

Chapters .... how do I write the chapters if this is a book...? I have so many thoughts that come to me... I write down the main thoughts of all the thoughts that I have. ....Do I expand on and add to those thoughts?? To read, think about and re-read for respectability to all people.

It feels like I could read the whole book in minutes, it seems as though I know it by heart. I must speak to all men and I must give ideas and thoughts to all people to enrich their lives.

There is probably some more additional deep thoughts here for some of those who call themselves Christians. And what we proclaim requires a responsibility from us to think wisely before we speak.

The fool is full of many words and sometimes maybe we all speak more than we should have, and those we speak to hear none of it.... Actions,... What do people hear in the actions we speak??

Often times' religious people get away with just speaking many, many words among themselves and others applaud them for their flowery tongue.

Sometimes it seems as if they are caught up with 'Monkey see, Monkey do' in their own little world that just pleases and impresses those in their own little group.

These people seem to be just hypocritical to other people who observe their self-righteous, pious actions, and as a result others completely miss the message of Gods gracious love for us.

...... It is our actions with or without our words that leave the deepest, most lasting impression.

Forward .... What additional thoughts would I write in a forward to the book......?..... *'This is written to all people, my thoughts and my feelings, my beliefs and my actions.'*

Some of my dearest friends proclaim themselves to be 'agnostics,' and I love them for who they are themselves as my friends. Sometimes I think they are 'better off' ....for the *present moment....*than those who just *'say'* they are Christians and deceive *themselves,* ....and *others.*

It is a terrible thing to think that the world hates you. I felt terrible when I thought Pastor Jim hated me. His letter has helped to change that feeling. I am wondering how many people in the world feel lost like that, and that nobody loves them, not necessarily that anyone hates them, just.... That nobody loves them.

The Tunnels Of Life

Maybe Pastor Jim will now help me one day with my Dearest, my *Kjærest.* Whatever is going on that I am unaware of, I do not think it is Pastor Jim's doing, I believe it is the Lord's doing for me to experience these things.

The midnight sun here in Norway seems to me to be an example of heaven, it never gets dark, the day never ends. Maybe one day the joy shall last forever also.

....And if the long summer day could be compared to Heaven, then the long winter darkness without electricity or candles to chase away the darkness, would be like a soft taste of Hell,...... without the torment. I cannot even begin to imagine only that, just darkness forever. ...

Alicia is like a light in that darkness of life for me. It is like the first time I went through a tunnel on the roadway in Norway.

Even the short ones seem long the first time you go through them. And then you see the 'Light at the end of the tunnel' and you know you are soon out of it.

Sometimes our problems and trials in life can seem like we are trapped, in a tunnel. We cannot turn to the right or the left, we must just continue on the path we are on.

Before entering the tunnels they post a sign telling you how long they are. Once in the tunnel they post signs telling you how many meters you have traveled into the tunnel, and once you have passed the midway point the signs tell you how far it is to the end of the tunnel so you know what to expect.

Simply knowing which side of the center of the tunnel you are at helps you to not panic and get out of the tunnel quickly if you have car trouble and have to walk out.

Lost In A Cornfield

Two times in my life I have been lost in the middle of the long rows of a cornfield, the memory of which is very similar to driving in a long tunnel.

With the first time, I am told that when I was a very young child of about a couple years of age, I wandered off from the house yard and walked down the gravel driveway and into a full grown corn field. I got lost in the rows and couldn't find my way out......

My Mom tells me that she had no trouble finding me following the sounds of my terrified screaming.

Fenced In

This resulted in my Dad building a 4 foot high, 2x4 inch wire mesh netting fence around the entire house yard, ...but, he used a piece of 5x5 inch spaced wire hog pen fencing to cover the pipe frame walk-in gate.

I climbed right up and over that, which resulted in my Dad attaching a smooth piece of tin over the wire so I couldn't climb over it.

My Mom has bought enough film for pictures over the years that I would have thought she might have had stock rights in the Kodak Company. Sure enough she was there with her camera the moment I failed my attempt to climb the new tin covered gate, and she took a picture of me hanging on the side of the gate screaming mad.

When looking at that old picture, I can almost see the frustrated angry red look on my face, in a black and white picture!

Failing To Learn From My First Mistake

The second time I vividly remember *choosing* to go into the scary tall corn rows out of curiosity, going in as far as I dared and then coming back out into the open. I did this repeatedly as I became more brave, going in farther and farther each time. Sometimes coming only halfway out and then going in further yet, until I lost track of which direction was the way was out!

…. I remember having a panic attack running back and forth trapped in the middle of the cornfield. I was old enough then that I did not want to scream or let anyone know I was lost for fear of getting a spanking from my Dad for disobeying.

'Lost At Sea'

In a similar, yet much more desperate feeling of helplessness, I know a little of what it must feel like to be lost at sea.

In February of 2006 I visited Hawaii for 3 days, later extending it to 10 days. Every day I helped one of my friends from Wisconsin that I had contacted there who happened to be building a new house for a lady on one of the eastern most shores of the Big Island, a few miles north of Hilo.

They set up my own tent for me on the jobsite next to two others living there. I also had the privilege of being a guest at two of the people's homes who were working on the house project, staying overnight with them truly experiencing a genuine Hawaiian lifestyle. Every day I enjoyed eating home cooked gourmet organic food and never needing to stay in a hotel!

After each day's work ended about 3 pm, my friend and several of the new friends I met working on the house project would take me on tours to different areas and towns around the island.

One day we took the whole day off and spent a good portion of the day later on the beach. Before they would let me go swimming in the ocean, they explained the rip currents, and what to do to stay safe. They also showed me how to dive straight into a big wave to experience it so I did not get slammed by one and go into a panic.

I saw one person swimming straight out away from the shore. I thought, if they can do it, so can I, so I decided to follow along. After a while we were separated a few hundred feet apart. I would see the person bobbing up and down as the swells and waves seemed to be getting bigger.

All of a sudden I completely lost track of them and decided that I had best swim back to shore.

As I turned around to swim back, I saw nothing but water, and waves, *big waves....and no shoreline! My first thought of panic* was that I had been carried out to sea in one of the rip currents they told me about!

Then I remembered being lost in the cornfield as a young child, and I was afraid to swim in either direction for fear of swimming farther out to sea.

I took a deep breath, and told myself to calm down. I decided to just ride the waves up and down and hope to see which direction the land was. I decided the most logical was that the waves were likely rolling *into* the shoreline, so I watched in that direction until the timing of the wave bulges allowed me to catch a glimpse of the shoreline. I remember what a beautiful sight that was.

As I started to swim back with a confidence of which direction *was the safe direction*, I thought about being lost in the cornfield, which did have an end to the rows and I could make it out again in as little time as it took me to get lost.

As I swam I also thought about people that have been shipwrecked, and lost at sea, some to be later rescued, and some who would perish at sea, alone.

Worse Than 'Lost At Sea'

Even with my few brief moments of panic seeing only water and big waves all around me, I know that I truly cannot enter into the hopelessness that some people in history have experienced knowing that they will likely perish at sea,…. and the moment that they realize that they must accept their fate, lost forever.

…… And I thought, worse than that of losing their physical life, how terrible would it have been for some of those same people to 'wake up' in eternity, and find out that eternity is true after all, even if they hadn't believed it before, and now it was too late to believe differently. (*Denying* the existence of eternity, Heaven and Hell,… *will not make it go away.….. 'if it is true,'* …..any more than *'believing'* it exists, would bring it into *'existence'* …if it didn't already exist.)

….Everything always seems ok, as long as we have some measure of hope. The sight of that shoreline was the 'road sign' that day for me that I needed to see, to give me that hope that I would soon have my feet on dry land again. It did not matter that I was probably a half a mile or more from it. I knew that I would soon be back on shore.

The roadway of life does not usually post those signs to let us know how long we may be in a given situation. We must look up, to see the light at the end of the tunnel ahead of us.

Songs In My Heart

A song just came to my heart, *'Softly and Tenderly Jesus is calling, calling for you and for me,'*... And then the words to the rest of the verse switched in my mind from English to Norwegian for the last words of the phrase to calling, *'Oh Venn, komme hjem.'* (Oh Friend come home) I sang these verses over and over in my thoughts silently in my mind.

Then the words of the song in my mind changed a little, the first part in English and the second part Norwegian. The words were now, *'Softly and Tenderly Jesus is calling, calling Min Kjærest, komme hjem.* (My Dearest, come home).'

These words also repeated themselves over and over in my mind. My first thought was of my Kjærest, Alicia,... Yes my Dearest come home, how I yearned for Alicia, for her daily presence.... And then I thought of Jesus saying those words, *"Min Kjærest Komme Hjem."* How he was saying that to every person on the face of the earth.

Then thinking of Alicia, new words in Norwegian seem to fit that tune. "Jeg er din Kjærest, Kjærest du er min, kommer hjem." (I am your dearest, Dearest you're mine, come home.) The words in Norwegian seemed to have a passion that I could not express fully or experience completely in English. Like a yearning or groaning that fails to produce words in any language.

Message In Norwegian

With thoughts of my Jesus, came also these words in Norwegian, *"Jeg gi min liv så du også kan live. Jeg Elsker du Meget og vent du vil se. ...Du må nå tro på meg"*........(I gave my life so you also can live. I love you very much and wait you will see. ...You must now believe (trust) on me.)

This was the first time the Lord spoke to me in my thoughts in Norwegian. It carried a much deeper impact for me that the thoughts about him came in Norwegian, and that he was reminding me of what I already knew that he gave his life for me that I might live forever, and that he loved me.

…. And,…That I must now believe on him in a trusting, different level of trust… my situation (with Alicia) was out of my hands,… I could only wait on him for his plan.

Some of the Norwegian words like 'Kjærest,' (chairrrest) translated directly is 'Dearest,' have taken on a new meaning entirely its own for me. I knew the word and how it was used in different situations, but,… I had locked it into my heart that it referred only to Alicia.

You can have only one Kjærest. The one that is above and beyond all the rest put together. For me, that would be my dearest, Alicia.

When we are with the Lord, *Alt Bli Bra.* (All is well) Both here and hereafter.

You cannot teach what you have not learned. I am learning all of these things for a reason.

When or if,… if or when,… I am back together with Alicia I will have complete contentment. We must learn to be content with what we have now that we may experience complete contentment with what we may have later. ….'*Be ye still, listen to and hear him*'….. I must learn to enjoy the timeout I have now.

Love Songs

Love songs generally seem all one and the same to me in content and yet all of us have one or more favorite songs. Love songs written by men about the woman, or women they have loved are easy for all of us to understand. Love songs written by women about the man or a man in their life are likewise also easy to understand.

When we attach the words of those songs to a specific person in our life, the songs become our favorites holding those special feelings up on a pedestal. The emotions well up in our hearts and overflow as tears in our eyes.

For some people who have not yet met the love of their life, these songs are held in their heart as Cinderella or Prince charming, waiting like a quest to be found. And once found, we need look no farther.

For me it was exactly the same with the gospel songs. For many years they were just religious songs to me, but when I understood how much that I was loved, they became very special to me.

When I realized that I was the object of his love, he became the object of my love in return, and likewise my search for understanding was fulfilled.

A new song that has been playing in my thoughts:

Met a young woman, was the one for him.
He did not listen to her every day, and then discovered she went away.
Everyone loved her, even all of his kin.
Little foxes, they spoiled the grapes, something little is all it takes.
So listen my friend to what I say,
Take a look at that woman you're married to and I will tell you what to do.
Love her morning, noon and night, soon you will know that this is right.
Rub her feet and back, do her fingers too, she will now respond to you.
Money don't buy what you can give.
It's little things that put the light in her eye, and someday she will ask you why.
……… "Lord, care for Alicia in the gentleness of your love, Amen."………

I am just thinking of her. Sometimes we pray with our head and our heart, sometimes with only our head or the most sincere, just with our heart... that which comes from deep inside.

Perspectives

Similar to Pastor Jim, sometimes maybe we act in what seems to be in the best interest at the time, without full information, ... or having only half of the story

Life, ... and what seems to be reality in life can sometimes maybe be only an illusion of what is actually true or not true.

I am looking at Reinsfjell and there is snow on the side of the mountain in a spot that gives the illusion that there is an enormous hole in the side of the mountain making it appear as if I can see clear through to the other side and it appears to match the clouds that are also over the top of the mountain.

Like work, a task, or a situation before us, take care of the worst first, that which takes the longest and everything else is easier and easier.

On the things that we do not understand, or that we can do nothing about, we must just accept what is, deal with it the best we can and wait and see how things turn out.....

Thinking about Pastor Jim.... I'm sure it is the Lord's plan to give us understanding of each other.

Any man can fall and we need a safety net. It is easy to understand that a man working in a high place should have a safety net in place should he fall, to save himself.

Any man can also fall spiritually, emotionally or ethically. We need a safety net there also. It can be written words that give us guidance or a close friend or brother that we can trust to give us good advice.

Women do a much better job of searching out a trustworthy friend than most men do.

If three people are seeking God's will for them in life it will happen.

Always say "I love you" last, if there's not another chance, ... Like Jeremy and Kristie, or my Grandma Olga.

We learn from and can appreciate success fully experiencing failure. We must want something first to appreciate it when we have it, be it a love or salvation. Appreciate having something by wanting it first.

Thinking about the words *'Every knee shall bow and tongue confess that Jesus is Lord to his glory'*. Wondering what others think when they read that?

Many times in life we have heard someone make a statement, or read something in a book or newspaper and we have all responded, well I don't believe that, ……..and later we say to ourselves, *WOW*, …. it's true after all.

Show Love like no other…………. And, simply show Love to others.

Thinking of Jeremy and Izzy… Jeremy yearned for the best for his daughter. Jesus yearned for the best for them. Maybe we just can't always see or understand everything, from our side of the fence. Many times we just don't have answers in this life for things that happen in our lives.

Jesus spent 33 years apart from his Father, in that time he was 'physically absent' from his Father's presence and yet present in thoughts and prayer and a spiritual connection, on earth he was maybe just 'absent' in those moments of prayer from the 'physical self' as I can best understand it.

For me, It's all about what I am able/or not able to do for Alicia….. likewise as he does for us,…………. it's about what he wants to do for us if we will let him…….. How many of us have had a 'restraining order' against the Lord from contacting us??………………

One day I said to Alicia, "It seems as though you're holding back." Alicia replied, "Of course I'm holding back." …….. I knew she was holding back a total commitment to me, in case I failed to complete the things that I needed to do and she had to let me go…….. She had to hold back to protect her heart.

Are we as Christians holding back from loving the Lord because we haven't experienced a commitment to do so yet? …… We can be trusting him safely in salvation and still not be committed to a relationship of daily communication with him.

The Holy Spirit is like a friend on your behalf…….. Will Pastor Jim be that for me?

Forgiveness, Commitments

Alicia can do no wrong in my sight. The day we were sanding the floor, she became extremely upset because the sander blew the electrical circuit breaker for the hot tub and she was beside herself with anxiety that her hot tub would freeze.

The *moment* I realized she was so upset, ….. *I knew in that moment,* that I would never have a fight or argument *about anything* with her because I *chose* in that moment not to ever respond in any confrontational or argumentative nature.

I choose to hold her blameless in anything and everything. I have a spirit of compassion and forgiveness in my heart for her that preempts anything that could happen.

We as Christians can 'do no wrong' in Jesus' sight. We cannot lose our position in him because we did not establish it. He *chose* to forgive us *in advance* for everything. He sees us as being perfect in his sight in himself, through himself, and we *can choose* to accept his gift. He made the commitment to us first.

Relationships are commitments. A marriage is a commitment. Living in both Norway and America I have observed different perspectives on relationships and marriage. In America we view marriage as being committed to our relationship. And yet we all know that some of those relationships in marriage have failed, myself included.

I have Norwegian friends who are not married and yet they are committed to relationships in which they raise families and exhibit total commitment to their relationships. I have observed and know beyond the shadow of a doubt that some of my unmarried Norwegian friends are far more committed to their relationships than many of my legally married friends in America.

Commitment to a relationship is above and beyond the piece of paper that says a person is married. A marriage license of a certainty does provide certain legal responsibilities, obligations and privileges.

Some of my married friends could acquire valuable perspectives observing the commitments I have noticed in some of my unmarried Norwegian friends who obviously have made permanent commitments to each other.

I told Alicia of my desire for commitment to her three hours after we met in the church hallway. I was delighted with her mutual response of feeling the same.

I remember the different moments in the following weeks that I silently made commitments to myself concerning Alicia … For better or worse. My present situation has not put my commitment to the test …. It has only confirmed it to me.

Enjoy The Moment

Our good memories are part of our desire for more in the future. Songs on the radio or the melodies played through the thoughts of our mind, recall those memories. Songs serve a purpose both in the singing of love songs in our hearts and in the proclaiming of God's love in his heart for us in the gospel songs.

Jesus always used parables and situations to help us understand his message of Love. Our own life experiences are like parables and examples that can serve the same purpose and often they are cemented fast in our memories so that we can continue to learn from our experiences.

July 3, mid-morning. We have fantastic weather that has come today and I am eating my breakfast out on the balcony this morning.

Every day is a good day and some days are better than others and every day that God has made is good. With every day, …. I must be content in it … and whatever the day holds.

This is the experience of a lifetime that you want to last for a lifetime, preferably with my Kjærest.

It is 80° at 10 o'clock in the morning, and yet the mountains still have snow left on them. From my place on the balcony everything in the surrounding area is still and quiet. There's a light wind that brings cool and refreshing air in the warm morning.

As I listen to the sounds of nature around me I can hear the occasional crow squawking. The faint sound of a car's tires on the highway more than a mile from here, slowly fade away, it is a pleasant sound. The leaves on the trees nearest me are moving gently in the breeze. As I concentrate on the stillness around me I can now hear the faintest of sounds.

As I look down from the balcony at the house yard below I see Jacko's doghouse standing empty, for some years now….. He is only a memory now.

I remember one night during my first trip to Norway, Ola saying to Jacko, "På Plass!" Jacko *instantly* went and laid down under the desk in the kitchen.

I thought *'Uff da, that dog understands Norwegian better than I do!'* …. It is the only time in my life that I can ever remember being jealous of a dog.

I remember the time when he and Pussycat laid on the balcony completely contented. The cows, dogs and cats live in a wonderful world, worrying about nothing.

There are flowers on the table on the balcony. With my feet resting up on a stool, I am enjoying the simple beauty of the flower petals and as I'm thinking of this, the Sun passes between two clouds and warms me with its direct rays.

While I am enjoying the fragrance of the flowers in the air I breathe, the Sun continues to caresses my skin with its warmth. I am lost for a little in my contentment of the moment, until I enjoy this 'moment' again the next time.

The Sun also gives pleasure to my eyes as I observe the patches of sunlight that move across the mountain on the other side of the fjord highlighting and drawing my attention to places on and beside the mountain like a spotlight highlighting the singer of the concert.

It brings back to my memory one day some time ago when I was driving back home here and I was on the highway across the fjord from the farm.

I looked over Karihavet on a cloudy day to see only one small patch of sunlight peeking through the clouds, and it was centered exactly and only on Ola and Martha's farmstead. It was a special experience for me and one of the times I really wish I would have had a camera in my hand in that moment.

All of the small places seem special and different as my attention is drawn from one spot to another, while the focus from the patch of sunlight keeps shifting and shifting and shifting. I embrace the view of each moment, for in the blink of an eye the scene is lost as the next appears.

I think of each moment that I was in the presence of my Kjærest Alicia. Life moves on like the spotlight, you must pay attention so you miss nothing and take everything in.

I think of my son growing up, and now my Grandchildren,... Enjoy the moments while they are present.....The next time that I sit here most of everything that I am looking at will still be the same... *Will I still be the same?*

Maybe, we must hunt for the best things in life. Many of the same things that we can now appreciate have always been there, but we just have not noticed them until now. We must open our eyes and pause long enough to appreciate the little things in our life that are more important than the big things.

Often I have been riding in the car with either my Norwegian friends or my son Chris, all of whom are avid and excellent hunters and they will say, "Look at that!" They saw the Big Buck standing next to the trees in the grass and I did not notice it.

Why would we want to pay money for what we can have for free?.. ....Maybe you won't ever have the chance again. Everything in life that costs money, either gets used up, wears out, or requires maintenance.

Of the things in life that are free, most of them are always free, with no strings attached. The warmth of the sunshine, coolness of the breeze, the pleasure of the beauty in nature, friendship between ourselves..... and The great gift of God's love to us in his Son.

It is all there whether we are aware of it or not. Have you ever been loved by someone, and you were not aware of it at the time? How does it make you feel when you find out that someone truly loved you? Doesn't it make you feel special? What if you never found out?.......

I guess it wouldn't matter then, because you would never know. It would have no positive or negative effect on you, it would not change your life from whatever you were experiencing at the moment....... But, what if?... you found out later,... after it was eternally too late, and you could not go back to when it would matter.

Foresight is the ability to use your imagination and logic to contemplate the possibilities that exist and oftentimes predict the likely outcome of a given situation. The choices are always ours, to hide your love, or to show your love. To reject love or to receive love, be it personal or spiritual.

We can embrace love and receive more, or some people reject it and miss the experience, together with the blessings it holds, and instead they experience feeling loss and emptiness.

Always Hope For More

Regnsfjell at 3000 feet stands majestic, like a Kings palace. As I look at it, it seems to represent the greater things in life that I have yet to experience...... to conquer the mountain, to experience the experience of going there, the climb, the exertion, the elation of the view from the top. …...

In all of the years I have been coming here to Norway I have not been up there yet, even though I look at Regnsfjell every day, except when fog, rain or snow hide it from my view.............maybe there is a reason why I haven't been up there yet.

Perhaps it represents to me the joy that is yet to come in my life, and greatest things in my life that are waiting for me, something to look forward to, something to hope for.

The Crown of Life, and a crown in life. He is the Crown of my Life and Alicia is the crown of my heart's experience in this life. Like the top of the mountain, He is the top of everything, and Alicia is the top of this mortal life for me. I have experienced both of those mountaintops.

3rd of July. 11:11am I have stopped for a coffee break, and made myself a cup of Gano coffee, it tastes good and it is supposed to be good for you. I am just enjoying the moment. .... Whenever I stop for a coffee, it seems as though my mind goes through a million thoughts.

Sometimes I just think about nothing for a few moments to clear my head and refocus on the most important things in life....... Jesus turned none away and so we should befriend all men.

Thinking back to the first two Sundays in December, at Pastor Jim's church. I realize now that it was God's plan even if it did not fit what I thought was God's plan at that time. The things that were happening just did not make sense to me. I am beginning to understand why everything has happened..... or *had to happen* the way things did.

The land of Norway is a little like being in heaven for me, as far as I can comprehend being human. Is a place I always wanted to go, a place I wanted to dwell in.

The distant mountains create the touchable space in between them. From where I am standing, looking into the sky on a clear day it is impossible to have any comprehension of distance.

The space between the mountains from my point of view gives me that comprehension of space, like looking into a small bowl or a large bowl, it is easy to comprehend the difference in volume. The space is enormous, still and quiet, and yet exciting at the same time.

The enormous still life photograph of nature is brought alive by the dancing of the water in the sunlight, all thanks to the invisible wind that moves across the waters with a spirit of life all its own. It can be still and warm in the sun and a few seconds or minutes later the gentle wind brings comfortable cool air. This is absolute perfect pleasure sitting here experiencing the warm sun and cool air together.

I could sit here the entire afternoon, just to stop and think, and to 'stop' thinking for a few moments just to enjoy the pleasure of this day. It helps me to become more and more patient as I wait for the future to unfold.

The most important perspective in my future now, is to wait for the chance that Alicia may become my bride...... I just realized this moment how much Jesus is anxiously and yet patiently waiting for his Bride. He gave himself for his Bride..... With Alicia I surrendered everything to her will. That was the best I could do for her, when I could do nothing for her.

July 3rd 7 PM. I have an absolute certain hope in Alicia and myself and in the meantime I have an absolutely perfect life, even in her absence. I have experienced perfect, and the perfectness that I have experienced because of knowing Alicia makes everything else perfect, ... knowing that I have missed nothing in life.

My life is full of completeness, and with a yearning in my heart I look forward to more of that completeness.

I understand how Jesus is looking forward to his bride, when together, we will be together forever. It is written he is preparing a place for us. I am preparing a provision for us also.

I am in the store and noticed a small flask of water for 15 crown, nearly 3 dollars! Something we can have for free and yet we should pay so much for it?? Salvation is free, love is free, friendship is free.

Thinking about how freely Pastor Jim embraced me as a Christian and a friend that first Sunday morning at his church, and then on Wednesday night when I went up for a men's Bible study, I felt so rejected, despised and accused.

I feel so embraced by him now that he signed his letter *Respectfully, Pastor Jim'*. I think I understand a little bit of how Jesus must've felt when he was rejected by the authorities of the synagogue, he was railed at and despised and I think I felt a small portion of the feelings he must have experienced.

As I'm walking on the road now and climbing the hill, I'm looking down as I walk, and I realize I need to look up and out to see everything. When I look down I only see what is immediately around me, and it is like a personal situation, if we only look at it, we don't see the bigger picture, only our present situation.

The Whole Truth Helps Focus Our Life

A Facebook Post asked, 'What was People's agenda, … money?'.…..……... What is our agenda?.... What is our purpose and motivation to anything and everything we do???

I have taken no money when I speak or sing. It is my responsibility to earn money, just like Paul did not take any money either, he was a tent maker. We always give what we have to give, for free.

I am alone on the mountain sitting on the backside of it. Thinking about that Jesus went up on the mountain to pray. It is quiet here, no distractions. It is a place we can be in prayer with no one to interrupt, no noise. Alone, at peace and concentration on our thoughts. Love, …. Life, ….and Hope.

My greatest hope of all is in Christ. My greatest hope for this life is in Alicia. Jesus is an absolute certain hope (assurance) to all Christians who know him and it is his desire that everyone would come to understand who he is.

To explain my certainty to others that they may better understand, I would say I am as certain as I can be about my eternal security, as certain as if I were already there, because he provided it as a gift for me, and has the same gift for you.

I am as certain as I can be about Alicia and me, from a human perspective, at least from my perspective. … Just thinking, if someone told Alicia right now under the present circumstances, how much I really care for her and that I have no interest in searching for anyone else now, and that I am content to wait and see what the future holds for us.,…... Would it make her mad?... or scared of something unknown or uncertain to her?.... Or perhaps filled with joy in her heart, to find out she is so loved.

So much misunderstanding, on everyone's part, it seems that everyone has only half the truth or part of the truth. The rest is assumed, and that can lead to complete misunderstandings, or completely inaccurate assumptions and conclusions.

Again it is like the woman at the well, when Jesus asked her to go and bring her husband, and she answered, 'I have no husband.' Jesus said to her 'you have answered truthfully you have no husband, for you have had five husbands, and he who you have now is not your husband.' She then knew that Jesus *knew* the *whole truth* about her.

Sitting on the mountain top helps give you a perspective of the whole picture, just like the whole truth.

Standing within the forest, you can only see a few trees near you. Even in a small clearing you still only get a small part of the big picture.

Only standing on top of the mountain reveals all. Only the whole truth, tells the truth. Anything less leaves room for error.

When Satan confronted Jesus on the mountain top he said fall down and worship me and all this shall be yours. They must've been able to see a good portion of the civilized world at that time, and it was a rather foolish statement and offer since ultimately it belonged to Jesus anyway.

From up on the mountaintop here in Norway even the big farms look small, big tractors look small, and big houses look small, and insignificant. Yet it is so still in this giant space between the mountains that I can hear the faint ringing of a sheep bell far off........ It is ironic that the smallest of things such as the bell on a sheep is the only thing in addition to the sounds of nature that I can hear.

I looked back and almost walked off the path... feeling a bit dizzy,... is this the same way Back?? It looks different looking at it from 180° coming down without the sun shining and it seems to be as hard as going up.

Maybe I can take another lesson from the sheep, and men that have gone before me, in following the worn footpath, the proven one that has a measure of safety to it. If you got off the path, in the wrong place maybe a person could go over the edge and get hurt, or worse end up dead, or maybe you just can't find your way back onto the path.

.... Slowly....making progress slowly. ....It is the same with success, and anything in life, like a rock, It may be hard to move. .... But keep at it and you will succeed.

Some Things Are Nothing And Some Are Everything

A person, it is all about a person, only Christ for me for salvation, I see only Alicia for me in love. The farm means nothing, money means nothing, nothing can replace either in each perspective.

It is written, *'There is nothing comely about him that when we see him we should desire him.'* It is just because it is him and what he means to us, what he has done for us, that makes him who is.

It is not that Alicia is more beautiful than other women or not, it is that she's the most beautiful to me, because I have seen past her physical beauty straight into her heart, and I've never been the same since.

I still wonder what happened........ It is written, 'Beware of the little foxes that spoil the grapes.'.... The smallest offense can destroy......... What was it??....... What happened between Alicia and I...... ?????

Wholehearted Commitment

I will give up absolutely everything for Alicia. We can live in the same place or anywhere she wishes to. It doesn't matter if I work at a gas station, drive semi over the road, or anything else that can earn the money we need to have a comfortable living. I would give up any and every dream that I might have to share my life with Alicia if that were necessary .....

Although I do not feel called to do so myself, I can *fully understand* the devotion that some people have to commit their lives to missionary work, giving up the pleasantness we have in life here with a total focus on serving the Lord, by serving others in challenging living situations around the world.

Ever since the *moment* on the day I met her, for me it has always been about the *something special* there is about Alicia.

And likewise since the *moment I understood* and could see that Jesus died on the cross in my place it has always been about him.

There is not any other choice in each respective situation, ... she is everything for my hope in this life and He is everything for peace of mind with God to me for eternity.

It is easy to understand love between two human beings, one for another. The normal relationship is easy to understand by everyone, each one loves the other, and each one appreciates the other likewise.

The exceptional loves are the ones where one stops loving, ...or at least showing evidence of it, and the other person continues to love and show love even when there's nothing in return.

It is so ironic that the same people that console and support a brokenhearted man whose wife has left relationship of a marriage, are the same ones that tell a brokenhearted man to 'Get over it' when he loses his girlfriend to a breakup, ... Two men that perhaps go to the same church, being talked to by the same people.

Perhaps the second one was just as devoted and faithful to the relationship,. ..... Or possibly even more so, since there is no legal obligation to stay in the relationship, and perhaps no children to consider from that relationship that would be a additional reason to maintain the relationship. It is all about a personal relationship that can be with no other person and have the same effect.

My relationship with Alicia, and my relationship with the Lord, have a very similar perspective for me. With each my personal human relationship with Alicia, and my spiritual relationship with the Lord, they each in their own perspective or respect were the complete fulfillment of what I had been searching for at the moment I found each of them.

The perspective that I've been able to understand regarding each one to the other has filled my heart with contentment knowing that I have found a perfect, unconditional love in another human being and likewise a perfect spiritual contentment, fulfillment and security in Jesus.

I'm still anxious to be back to where I was with Alicia, if that is possible........ and at least I understand that I found what I was looking for. It is not that I just understand now what I had with Alicia, I knew it then, I knew it all along.

What brings contentment to my heart right now is that I have experienced your presence Alicia, even just memories of your past presence fills my heart with contentment and joyfulness, thus, making my life complete..... And it would be wonderful to add more of that completeness to the rest of my life.

Herredsdalen

I'm wondering what new understanding I may get today????..... We are on the way to the outdoor church service in Herredsdalen. It is so incredibly beautiful walking along the mountain lake on the way back to the end of the valley where the service shall take place.

Some small details are only seen one by one individually. You can look at a tree as a whole and then you can see the individual limbs and leaves. As I observed the birch trees growing along the lake in this valley, I remembered the first time I came to Norway in February of 1997 and I saw them growing along the train tracks on the train from Oslo to Oppdal, I thought, *'Wow!* .... *this looks just like Wisconsin!* Now I can see why my Great Grandpa moved to our area in Crawford county, ... it would have made him feel *'at home'* .... away from home.'

It was a new experience to see these beautiful white barked trees that are so common in Wisconsin where I grew up, to be part of the bigger picture of the beauty here in Norway and the trees seem even more beautiful with the backdrop of the mountains as I behold this beauty before my eyes.

Once you start to notice the small things of the big picture you start to see all of the small things.

I remember also another unique experience during my trip to Hawaii and my friends there insisted that I go snorkeling. I was thinking, *'Okay, I will do it just to say that I have done it.'* As I waded out into the water between the large rocks that stood as small islands, more than I could count, I picked out a large pool of water, put on my snorkeling mask and took a look beneath the surface.......

I was speechless when I beheld the beauty underneath in the sea, hundreds and hundreds of small fish, different sizes, shapes and colors, and the uniqueness in the different ocean plants and the coral. I stayed under for 45 min. to an hour and most of what I remember was the first few minutes of amazement as I beheld something that I did not have a clue that existed.

As I walked here now alongside the lake in this quiet and beautiful valley, I was not sure exactly what to expect and so I observed every little thing that I passed on the way in.

There is a small roadway parallel to the lake shore only a few feet from it, that runs back to the valleys end where the buildings stand that served as a 'Seter' (an old summer pasture milking farm) at the end of the lake, but the roadway is little used. The common access for visitors is to park their vehicles and walk back here, or to the top of Skarven, the highest mountain in this area.

While our purpose today is to go to the church service, which is done once a year in this special valley, it is a spiritual experience in itself just to walk in the nature here in Norway.

As I contemplate all of this, every little thing I see seems to speak to me spiritually of my walk in life. As we began walking from the parking area we took a shortcut down to the small roadway cutting across soft marshy land.

There were small wooden shipping pallets laid out across small little ditches and a small foot bridge crossing a small stream. More small pallets and things to walk on made it easier to walk in this area where the ground was so soft. A way had been prepared in advance for me by strangers to me, who were motivated to do so for their own benefit, their friends and… strangers as well.

As we walked along the way this Sunday morning, it spoke to me in my heart of Jesus, who prepared the way for me as well. The difference was when he did so, he was a stranger to me in my heart, but I was known to him who was my friend and loved me, even though I did not know this at the time.

Likewise the examples I see for this physical walk are applicable to my spiritual walk. The way we are walking on has been used by others to avoid the pitfalls along the way. The grass along the pathway looks firm and yet is unpredictably soft, step in the wrong place and you can go in over your ankles up to your knees. The deeper the hole, the bigger trouble you are in.

It is best to step on rock if possible, they always support you. Yes, He is a rock, and he will always support you. The good path we are walking on is parallel to all the pitfalls, which are always changing. Even the old wood planks laid out across the mud are a welcome sight, anything to keep me out of the mud hole.

In some places the rain has washed the top of a rock off clean and I am glad to see it because I know that I can confidently step on that solid rock, which instantly reminds me of my Savior and how he is always there for me, like a rock.

And yet in the war between the water and rocks, water eventually always wins in the nature, when the rock remains exposed to the force of the water, such as underneath a waterfall,….. it will eventually wear away the rock.

It is the same with Temptations, if they continue long enough they will likely have an effect on that rock ….You and me. I fully understand that Jesus is the only Rock that will never erode or diminish for any reason.

After we walked past the soft areas onto a solid and safe road, I am able to turn my attention to enjoy the scenery, be aware of, and feel the cool fresh breeze with little else on my mind. I did not notice that when I was on a poor path and had to watch every step……..

How many bigger and more important things have we all missed out on in life because we were taken up with the smaller short term issues in life. When we look up and out beyond our present situations, we are able to see the bigger picture of life, and eternity.

Walking along this still quiet lake reminds me of what is written, *'Come beside the still waters.'*

The smell of sheep hangs lightly in the air, and sheep bring to my thoughts, the thought of a lamb, and the thought of a lamb, brings me to the thought of him, who was called *The Lamb*, …who sacrificed himself for me. I hear the gentle tinkling sound of a sheep's bell as I quietly walk along….. You always know where they are by the sound of their bell.

I have, and must continue to take a stand in my life to proclaim who I am, and where I stand … to make my presence known, just like the sheep. Life is what happens along the way, it is not a destination, it is truly a path we walk.

The Church Service

The sermon, ….. Will I miss any of the message today?….. because of course the entire service is in Norwegian. As much as I have learned, I do not always understand all of the conversation.

Perhaps that's the same as for some people sitting in a church service of their own native language and they don't hear all of what's being said.

Spirituality is about matters of the heart, not just the sight of the eyes, or what we hear in our ears. Songs they have chosen for today relate a good message of the gospel of God's love.

Likewise I am enjoying the message in the sermon. The church service is held between the old buildings of the Seter, the summer farm used here years ago. We are sitting upon board planks laid out on the grass in rows like church pews. The boards seem to give a little organization to the impromptu service.

The thing that speaks the loudest to my heart is the presence of the sheep grazing on the fresh green grass all around us, and to see a little lamb epitomizes the story of the gospel. The quiet and gentle sheep, and especially the little lamb reminds me of our quiet and gentle Savior.

Enjoying The Experience

I am sitting here together with many friends and neighbors from this area. I actually know the majority of the people gathered here today. I am sharing this outdoor experience with them and at the same time my heart is in a world all its' own as I look upon the beauty of the mountains that extend U-shaped around all three sides of us at the upper end of this Valley.

We are not quite at the very end of this enormous, somewhat flat wide valley. We are just far enough from the end of it so that both the sides and the very end of the valley appears to be equal distance from where I sit, so that as I look at one side of the mountain and gaze slowly around to the end of the Valley and to the mountains behind me it is one long beautiful panoramic picture.

It speaks to me of the Majesty of God, the enormity of his universe and how small our little gathering is in this vast Valley. I am one with the Majesty of God in Nature here today exactly the same as I believe most every Norwegian is most every time they take a fjelltur and I feel that I am physically in the presence of the Lamb, symbolically portrayed by the sheep and the little lamb standing beside the fence.

Perhaps that is indeed the contentment that likely all or at least most Norwegians find in a fjelltur. Everyone I know in Norway seems to have a deep appreciation for the beauty and experiences in the nature. Their genuine appreciation and perspective of the nature reminds me of an experience I had more than 20 years ago after a church service one evening.

Coffee At Ethel's

It was quite common for several of the people to stop at Ethel's house for coffee afterwards. We usually had coffee and chocolate chip cookies or some other snack to go with the coffee.

We usually sat around the table in the kitchen, sometimes for twice as long as the church service lasted further discussing the thoughts of the evening meeting. There was always plenty to talk about.

One particular night more people came than could sit around the table and we moved to the living room. We had a special chocolate dessert cake that evening that was especially delicious.

After tasting it I said "Ethel, this chocolate dessert is delicious." Ethel replied, "Oh don't thank me, thank Carolyn, she made it." I turned to Carolyn, the wife of my best friend from high school who was sitting next to Ethel, and said "Carolyn, this cake is delicious." She graciously and quietly said "thank you."

I had complemented Carolyn two times. The first time when I directed the comment towards her mother-in-law Ethel, Carolyn was complemented indirectly even though I directed the comment toward Ethel.

Carolyn knew she made the cake and the complement was at first indirectly received. Since I knew Carolyn, and that she had made the dessert, I turned to her and complemented her again directly. She had now received two complements in a row.

I then turned and said to Carolyn's husband, "Daryl, do you realize how fortunate you are to have such a good cook for a wife!" Carolyn was now indirectly complemented again for a third time.

It is the same when people truly appreciate the beauty of the nature. When anyone is thankful for or truly enjoys the beauty of the Nature in creation, God receives praise and appreciation indirectly, because he knows he made it. When we know him personally we can turn to him and thank him directly.

If we tell someone else later or show them beautiful pictures of breathtaking views in the mountains or of a tropical paradise, God is complimented again indirectly even if the people showing the pictures are not aware that they have proclaimed and praised Gods handiwork in the Nature.

... I am personally convinced that it is possible that God indirectly receives more of a compliment, which is a form of praise, in peoples' genuine appreciation of the beauty in Natures creation, even from someone who claims to be an atheist, but, they are truly appreciative of the Nature,...... than he does from some of those who claim to be Christians, and may or may not be, but are caught up with their own self-righteousness and their 'praise or thankfulness' for some things is simply elegant words directed toward others, that they might be impressed by what they are saying, and the true praise that God deserves, is lost in someone's self-righteous arrogance.

Memory Triggers

My friend Steinar, Ola's Brother, is smoking as he walks along with us as we are leaving. It is the one smell that decisively overcomes the odor of the sheep.

Neither of the smells offends me. I grew up on a farm where over the years I experienced the smells of dairy cows, hogs, chickens, and horses, a dog, cats and the terrible smell of pigeons in silos. Each of the animals simply having their own unique odor easily identifiable when you are accustomed to it.

Different smells, pleasant or unpleasant, can each trigger memories of the past for each of us. The good smell of fresh baked bread takes me back to my childhood days as does the smell of new-mown hay drying. The fragrance of flowers or a special perfume often can take us back to thoughts of a special person in our life, now or from the past, bringing those memories into the present.

My Dad

Although I have seldom smoked myself, my father smoked. The fragrance of cigarette smoke always brings back warm memories of my Dad to my heart.

My father Arlin passed away on the Saturday before Christmas in 1998. He had been on kidney dialysis for four years. He continued to smoke throughout his life and the last 10 months of his life he depended on a wheelchair. Because of his health condition he would occasionally fall asleep, even while he was smoking a cigarette.

Because of this he and my mother decided they needed to keep the matches away from his reach whenever she was gone. He would sometimes simply hold a cigarette in his hand or in his mouth even though it was not lit. It was simply a matter of safety after he had fallen asleep a couple of times and burned two holes in the sofa.

On Thursday, the 17th of December, just two days before he passed away, at which time the thought never crossed my mind that he had so little time to live, I stopped by my parents' home for a cup of coffee and to say 'Hi' because I had come to town for a part I needed on the farm.

Fortunately for me, Mom had just baked a large fresh batch of chocolate chip cookies that went very well with the coffee. After a short visit and several cookies with my coffee, I told Dad I was in a hurry and needed to get going. He said, "Say, before you go, light me up a cigarette"....

That meant I would have to stay there until he finished the cigarette. ......It also meant I could eat more cookies!! We got caught up in a conversation that lasted much longer than the cigarette did. I looked at the time and said "I really need to get going."

By now, Dad said, "Light me up another cigarette before you go." So I did, and that meant *more coffee and cookies*!! Somehow we got caught up in a long conversation with things that happened years ago on the farm.

Quite a long time into his story, I looked at the clock, abruptly stood up and said "I HAve to get going Dad." Dad said to me, *"You just SIT back DOWN!* I'm not finished with my story yet. Go get some more cookies and another cup of coffee and light me up one more cigarette." So I did all of that, and he finished his story.

As I got up to leave, he had one more request of me. He said, "Will you help me to stand up before you go? *I have to stand on my own 2 feet."* I took hold of his hand as if we were going to shake hands, and put my left hand behind his arm to assist him up from the sofa.

As soon as he was standing, I let go of his hand and he just stood there by himself and said "Ohhh this feels good, *Ohhhhh this feels good,.....* I think maybe by spring I can get back to *walking again*!!'

Thoughts And Memories To Appreciate

Yes, I have a somewhat fond affection for the smell of cigarette smoke.... I would realize later, that *those three cigarettes bought me more than two hours more time to visit with my Dad,* and I had the privilege of helping him to stand up alone on his own feet, helping him experience the dignity of self-sufficiency, escaping the need of the wheelchair.

I never had a *clue* that he was *actually standing at the threshold of eternity, soon to enter into it* .....Yes, Thank You my Friend for the memories, by smoking that cigarette.

As we were leaving we all walked down to the edge of the water and I sat down at an old wooden table next to the beach.

I needed to enjoy and embrace this moment for long as I could. The large lake…. and the boat landing … the sun ….. which had now slipped partially behind some clouds …….and there was a gentle breeze. The Majesty of the mountains….. and the complex, yet simple beauty that lay before my eyes all around me.

I am thinking about how much I have enjoyed my time here in Norway…. I thought back to December of 08 when Alicia asked me, "And when do you go back to Norway again?"….. I replied "The 6th of January," and *immediately* I thought *'This is the end of my time in Norway,'* because I have finally found what I was searching for.

I knew that being with Alicia was more important than going back to Norway like I had been doing. As I thought about her now, I knew that if she would give me a call and asked me to come home I would be on a plane in the blink of an eye.

As I sat there yet at the old wooden table, I searched with my eyes to take in every little detail of the environment around me. Some children playing in a boat in a little harbor, the harbor is a safe place, every Hytte looks a little different, and yet the same, all a part of the picture in life.

As I'm walking back on the roadway the gravel under my shoes takes its toll with wear on the bottom of my shoes. And likewise the light wind causes the water on the lake to splash against the gravel laying on the shore, and the water eventually takes its toll on the rocks, simple cause and effect.

While everything has an effect on us, positive, … or sometimes negative if we fail to put things in a right perspective, we can choose to see all things in our lives as stepping stones to better understanding to our hearts and our minds for good.

…I must convert the talking I do with so many people to writing, so that more people may benefit from what I've learned from my experiences.

I noticed three large rocks near the edge of the water that are each about the size that would fit in a wheelbarrow. The three rocks remind me of the three small islands in Kari Havet, which each remind me of the Trinity, Solid and steadfast, each a symbol of refuge.

There are many different things to look at as I walk along, but there is always the smell of sheep, and again always reminding me of him who is the lamb.

Walking back I feel like I have a little experience knowing where to walk to avoid the pitfalls or soft areas along the path. Life experiences give us the same advantage to avoid the pitfalls, and the consequences thereof.

Quickly my thoughts abandoned the environment around me and my heart and mind is totally focused on thoughts of Alicia and the reality of her absence.

It is the communication that I miss the most, just being able to talk to her, even if only over the phone, from part way around the world. To know what she's thinking and understand how she feels......

One year ago today, Alicia and Marc were on their way coming to Norway to visit me for a couple weeks and I was eagerly looking forward to seeing both of them.

I was looking forward to getting married as soon as that would work out for us, ... the thought never crossed my mind that there was even a possibility of losing Alicia and Marc out of my life. They had truly become my family in my heart and I loved them both.

Alicia's absence from my life for me, is similar to the Lord's absence, in that after you have once experienced their presence nothing else can fill the void in either situation....

Most of us have loved someone in life, and some of us have lost something or someone. Perhaps some of us, or all of us can say that we could have had something or someone in life and we passed the opportunity up, only to realize later what we have lost, that which we never had.

I can imagine it would be like that for someone that passed up the love and forgiveness that God offers all of us in Jesus, and too late they realize they will never again have that chance in all of eternity.

My Three Little Birds

8:30 PM Fourth of July. We are done with the activities of the day and I have decided to take a walk in the forest. I'm just walking quietly up Vettafjell with thoughts of my Savior embracing my heart. I am one with him alone in the forest. I am enjoying a measure of peace and contentment in my heart and this time with him here in the presence of the nature he created seems like a small taste of heaven to me.

I have been walking quietly up the mountain, and I am in the area where the trees have become very sparse and widely scattered. The path on which I am walking is in a wide open area,......... And for the third time in my life God has laid a dead sparrow in my path immediately in front of me.

The first time this happened was almost 10 years ago. I was very heavy hearted about personal situation and I was feeling like I was lost and alone and no one cared about me, and it seemed that even God was not paying much attention to me and my troubles. I really, really felt alone and abandoned.

I was working on a combine preparing it for the harvest season and I had the combine parked halfway in the doorway to the shed. The large front drive wheels were parked exactly in the doorway leaving less than 3 feet between the tire and the shed post. I was carrying several parts inside the shed that had been piled up outside.

Each time I passed between the tire and the shed wall I always looked at the ground, careful not to step in some water puddles just outside the door. I had just carried one item in, set it down and was going back out of the door less than 30 seconds after I walked in.

As I walked out and looked down at the ground between the tire and the shed post, there lay a dead sparrow, exactly where I stepped every time. He was not there 30 seconds ago.

I knew that he had just died and fell to the ground. It is written, 'Not a sparrow shall fall to the ground but the Lord shall know it'........ And 'Ye are worth more than many sparrows'..... Even a single little sparrow was important to God's heart.

Instantly I knew the Lord was speaking to my heart, and instead of thoughts coming into my mind, he used the dead sparrow to speak louder than the words in my thoughts would've spoken. Something that was alive only a minute ago, now laid dead before me.

I felt that it was my fault that this little sparrow had to die just so God could use this example to me together with the words that are written about both the value of the sparrow and our even greater value in his sight.

As a child I was scared to death of the Rhode Island red roosters that used to chase us, and as much as I hated dirty stinky pigeons, ...and anything with feathers, I picked up this little sparrow and held him in my hands feeling that it was my fault, he had to die.

I walked outside of the shed door, walked about 10 feet and knelt down alongside the shed. With my bare hands I scooped away a little dirt next to the wall and then laid the little bird in the hole I dug for him and covered him up. It was the least I could do, and the only thing I could do.

The second time this happened was in December of 2009 just a short time after Alicia had completely broken it off with me with the restraining order.

I was both devastated with losing her and completely bewildered at how this had happened since the last time I spoke with her was when she returned my missed good morning call after she got to work to wish me a good day. There were so many unanswered questions……..

This second experience happened while I was working on the farm with Morten at the grain bins and I needed a certain kind of a wrench from the shop in the shed. I walked through the side door where the dump truck was parked with the nose of the truck just sticking through the doorway.

Again I had less than 3 feet to walk between the shed post and the front tire of the truck. Once more there was a water puddle, now with a thin coat of ice on it just outside of the doorway and I had to watch where I stepped.

I went into the shop, grabbed the wrench I needed and walked back through the doorway again looking down at the ground next to the iced over water puddle as I walked between the tire and the post, and,… for the second time in my life God laid a dead sparrow in my path to remind me that he loves me, …and I knew that he understood the sorrow that I was carrying on my heart.

I reached down and picked up this poor little dead sparrow. Because the ground was frozen I was unable to dig a hole to bury him and since I was in a hurry to finish what I was doing, the only thing I could do, was set the little bird aside behind the shed and cover him up with whatever I could find.

It wasn't much of a burial, but it was the only thing I could do for this little bird that had to lose his life, ….. just so that God could speak to my heart.

Both the first and the second sparrows were adult birds; they had lived some measure of a full life.

This third little bird was a very different experience for me. He was not an adult, but a large fledgling bird and had not even half fully gained his feathers.

I looked up, out and around me. I was quite puzzled; because there was no tree anywhere near where I was standing, just some short grass along the pathway. Where had this bird come from??

Both the first and second sparrows that God laid in my path to remind me of himself and his love for me were explainable in that they could have just been sitting over the doorway in each of the two different sheds and had simply died and fell to the ground landing exactly in my path.

Some other people could say that each of those birds in the doorway were coincidental. Personally I really do not believe in coincidence, I believe in purpose. I believe that things happen for a specific reason, either for myself or the benefit of others.

This third bird was more emotional for me in that there was absolutely no explanation for how this bird with no feathers could end up laying right in front of me on my path in this wide open area of the mountain.

Also it was obvious that it was freshly laid there, because this bird too was also warm and soft, not old, stiff and cold.

I am absolutely convinced for myself and my own purpose, that God's hand placed each of these birds in my path, because of the impact that each of them had to my particular situation at the time.

This large young bird seemed completely out of place where he lay, as out of place as a polar bear cub in the desert.

One thing I was sure of was that this little bird also was dead and I knew only God had power to give life to something that was already dead...

I was thinking of Lazarus as he lay buried in the tomb, and I would have, like those that stood there saw no hope of life in something or someone that was dead. ....

It would have been quite an experience to have been standing there that day with them and witnessed Jesus raising Lazarus from the dead.

Have A Focused Walk In Life

In the place where I'm walking now, ... I am not sure if I am on the correct path. In my uncertainty the obvious choice is to follow a well-worn path, in doing that you must trust where that path will lead you.......

I am thinking about the invisible path that each of us walks in life, where is it leading us? Are we on the road to happiness, personal, financial or academic success? And regarding our spiritual and emotional path, and success... Are we where we want to be?....

8:43 pm 4th of July Whichever path we are talking about, if we are not where we want to be, or believe that we are not where we should be, we need to take the first step. The journey of 1000 miles begins with but the first step. Take the first step and the next step will be revealed.

Walking on a worn and smooth path each step is easy, just put your foot forward, up and down repetitiously and you make progress with little effort or thought of safety.

Walking up a steep mountain path on uneven terrain, often every step must be chosen carefully to protect our legs, ankles and feet.

Walk the path on a high mountain cliff, and each step must be chosen carefully to protect your very life. We can ask ourselves, are we on a safe path in our spiritual walk?

The one single reason I know my love for Alicia is pure and genuine is because of how close it has drawn me to my spiritual walk with my Lord and Savior Christ Jesus. It is my passion and compassion for Alicia that has paralleled the understanding of my love for her, and His greater love for me.

Understanding the depth of my love and devotion to Alicia no matter what, has given me an even deeper emotional perspective of His love, commitment and sacrifice concerning me, for my happiness,… and for my salvation than ever before.

9:20 PM Fourth of July, I am about 100 meters up from Ola's cabin on the way to the top of Vettafjell. I'm walking on a very long rock and I can see exactly straight into Tingvollfjord. Somehow I find complete satisfaction in where I am at emotionally, physically and with everything I can see from here. I am totally enjoying the moment.

I've been walking and just looking out at the mountains and the several fjords in different directions that I can see from this mountaintop. I took my eyes off the path and I quickly drifted off course from where I wanted to be heading to the peak of Vettafjell, where I always sign my name in the book up there. I can see the pile of rocks where the mailbox is that holds the books where everyone signs their name when they've reached the top of the mountain.

It is that pile of rocks that helps refocus the direction of my walk. When we know what we are looking for, it is easier to find. ….Thinking of Jesus and his Love for me, always helps refocus the direction of my walk in life.

It is 9:30 PM It has taken me 1 hour and 20 min. to walk up from Ola and Martha's house. I am finally on top of the mountain after a slow and peaceful walk, without a single stop to rest. It does not seem like I put very much effort into walking to the top of the mountain. I just kept at it, and ended up on the peak. My signature in the book is the evidence that I made the trip.

Success,…. with anything in life is the exact same process, just keep going one step at a time and you'll one day find yourself on top looking down on or out over your success.

I am looking down at the still, quiet and yet powerful fjords, and the strong silent steadfast mountains. There is no sun out this evening. The atmosphere has a grayish color to it.

It is similar to what life without Alicia in it is like for me. Alicia's presence would brighten every day, rain or shine.

A Letter To Alicia And Marc

10:00 PM I am at the cabin………. God has to let us be by ourselves to purify our hearts to him. Think, …Just think,……………… I need to write a letter to Alicia and Marc.

My Dearest Alicia and Marc, It is Fourth of July today and I am sitting in Ola and Martha's cabin reading what we wrote almost 1 year ago. I have thought about us and everything we enjoyed last year. Alicia, all the way up the mountain I remembered how happy we were walking up and how happy it made you to see Marc running up the mountain not bothered by his asthma. And how happy he was to beat us up to the top. I recall with fondness the joyful laughter that filled this room as we laughed and laughed until you cried tears laughing about a chance of a chance of a chance to enjoy all of this. I never dreamed for a minute that a year later I would sit here as I am. It seems there is more than 2 million thoughts I yearn to tell you, and Marc likewise I have loved you also like my own son and I feel that began to really deepen April/May last year. I enjoyed not only your Mom's company, I truly enjoyed your presence as it made a complete circle of love between Alicia and I for me. When a man and woman get married it is the birth of a child between them that fulfills the bond of love between them and you did that symbolically for me. That you were and still are in a special way a permanent bond between the three of us in my heart for me. At this point today I have no certainty of what the future holds for us. I only know that I can trust my Savior and my God to give me the very best in life and you and your Mom are the best part of my life I have known. To the both of you I thank you for allowing me the privilege to be together with you and share the simple things of daily life. Work and success were always my priorities and I found that my greatest priority became getting to your house on time when I was invited for supper. I do not know today what the future holds and as a Christian I can only trust he has a plan. It is my hearts desire that he will bring us together again. And I already know that he has brought understanding of himself to my heart because of my love for you both. He has been able to reveal his greater love for me and all men. If and whenever this letter may get to the both of you. I want you both to know that my heart has always loved the both of you and never have I been upset or angry with either of you. Like gold in the fire is purified, so each thing that I have experienced has only shown me how endlessly deep my love for you both really was, and is, and will always be. Love Curt

10:57 PM Quiet, absolute quiet....only a few drops of rain on my jacket sitting outside on the balcony overlooking the fjord below me.... And the thoughts came to me from the Lord.......... *"Be still and listen to me........ Draw near to me, Dwell in perfect peace."* ....….........Oh to be at peace. ....*Ohhhh...to be at peace with Alicia!* ....and most importantly ... To Know, that I know.. that, *I Am at peace with God.*

What would it be like for Alicia to be here again? And spend a few days in this quiet?.... What would restoration be like?

260 Days

11:30 PM 260 days........ What is 260 days??? The thought and the number '260 days' was laid upon my mind. Is this something to do with the date of restoration?? 260 days from December?..in August?? Or.....

Are these the number of days I would miss out on being with Alicia each year if I were to drive semi? If I drove five days a week and were home two days a week, two days each week times 52 weeks equals 104 days. Subtracted from 365 days a year equals 261 days away from home each year.........hmmmm?? ...I'm still not certain what this means and I feel it means something significant.

Maybe instead of driving my semi as a business, I can sell something from home and be home all the time. .... Would we be married quickly?,.... And not have to dwell apart any longer?, ...or would we never be married, never be restored even as friends, and I would never have the pleasure and privilege of her company again in this life and only be restored in spirit once we are home in Heaven? Is this a revelation from the Lord that Alicia and I shall soon be restored??... or not?... Is this on my timetable or his?? It is written, *'A day is as 1000 years and 1000 years is as a day to the Lord'* .... Too much deep thinking for me for now.

Wandering

I feel like I'm wandering in the wilderness as I start my journey down the mountain from the cabin, and it feels symbolic, as if I am wandering in the wilderness of the emotions in my mind.

It is slightly dark and while I can see where I'm going everything looks a little different. I am familiar enough with this part of the mountain to not feel lost and yet it is a good feeling to find the path again, that familiar path that says I know exactly where I'm at.

The worst would be to be lost in a snowstorm. Snow covers your tracks in the blink of an eye and you may have no clue which way is north or south. It is good to have a compass that you may know the direction you are going. Good hunters and good sailors all know this, and sometimes your very life can depend on it.

Spiritually I'm thankful that I know my direction, even though I have been experiencing these sorrows of the heart so much of the time now. Thank you Lord Jesus for being the way the truth and the light, it is written *'No man comes to the Father but by me,'* which gives me life forever.

Pondering The Thoughts In My Mind And On My Heart

11:57 PM Back at the house again. A Facebook post: 'Tears of Restoration, ... be involved........ Softly and tenderly, Jesus is calling for you, and for me.' How many tears I have shed thinking about Vivian's post, thinking about happy tears of restoration to Alicia, and perhaps the 'tears' of happiness in God's heart the moment we are restored in our relationship to Him.

It is written *'I am tired of their tears.'*......... what does this mean??? ...... is the Lord 'tired' of listening to us cry?..... or is a better 'translation'/ 'interpretation',..... that the Lord is simply 'Sad' in his heart for our sadness??.... Does any of this fit with 260 days,?..... August, plus or minus????...........Hmmmmm….... or am I misinterpreting all of this?..

I must simply trust that whatever occurs in my life in the future is God's desired Blessing for my life…. 'Period.'

Wed FB post. 'The Old Rugged Cross' ……….. He laid down all things for me spiritually,…..in my capacity as a human being, I willingly laid down all that I could for Alicia's sake…..

I want to proclaim my love for Alicia in a similar manner as I proclaim my love for my Savior to the world….. It may help someone to understand Gods greater Love for them when they can understand the parallels of my human Love for Alicia, to God's spiritual love for us as our Creator.

……… The Lord has been having his time with me to teach me things that I did not fully understand, and I have been having my special time with Him. These words came to mind, '*It is finished*,'… the words that Jesus said on the cross when the payment for my sins was completed, ……and I know that my understanding is becoming more complete now. Everything is always best when it is finished or completed, nothing more to do and we can rest.

Thinking about songs on my heart that I know, "The Old Rugged Cross," "Savior of Sinners," "Man of Sorrows," "Rock of Ages,"… and,………. "I Walk Through The Valley"…….. With no fear of the future, I am learning to trust him better in my uncertainties in this life.

No matter what we go through on the highway of life, it comes and goes and we go through it, and for the most part we are always okay afterwards and……..Sometimes better off... and wiser.

So Many Things To Think About

FB post from the Fourth of July. 'You cannot worry yourself to wealth.'

I commented, "Very true, and wealth is most often thought of as money, while True Wealth is so much more. Do what you love doing best and as often as you can whether you make money or not….. And the money may well be in doing your favorite thing, either way you will be as happy and 'Wealthy' as you can be. ….. We need a given amount of money to live, and we can live abundantly with a lot of, or little money. …. We must just keep all of the thoughts of wealth in perspective, both for this life and for eternity."

FB Lake Geneva post; 'Memories.'

I commented, "Great memories of tomorrow are created today. May we all consider today what we want our memories tomorrow to be. May we live our life doing something good,... that will outlast it."

The news of a Facebook post from back home; There had been a bar fight in which a '16-year-old' was killed,.... How could that have happened???, .. *A 16 year old????*'

Another Facebook post; A canary hit someone's car and was killed….. and the driver was feeling bad about it…. I was thinking about my three sparrows that had lost their lives too.

In another post a young woman was having morning sickness and expecting a new baby around Christmas. I wrote to her, "The joy to come will make the morning sickness all worthwhile. Children are a gift enough."

Thinking again about Kristie and that she would likely give up every material possession she has just to hold Jeremy and Izzy one more time……. Oh my,.. so many thoughts,... someone going out of your life and NO hope…..

I reacted the same now as when I read of Jeremy and Izzy killed last May when the vehicle hit them head on. I felt the tragedy of their families loss as deeply as when I unexpectedly lost Alicia and Marc from my life.

FB post. 'Morning sickness again.'….. posted by the young expecting mother,…. A simple physical reaction by the body because of the pregnancy…

Thinking about other things that can make us sick to our stomach. News of untimely deaths from car accidents, heart attacks or terminal illnesses, …… families left in despair, with nowhere to turn ……… I have known so many to suffer losses, it makes me sick to my stomach.

I wrote: 'What has worked for me, to sooth both emotional and physical pain is singing out loud (or silently in my thoughts) favorite songs that embraced the tender memories I held in my heart.

The worst physical pain I have ever experienced was when the cap on a hot tractor radiator exploded when I touched it, instantly sending a one inch stream of boiling hot water up under my shirt sleeve of my left arm.

I immediately pulled up my shirt sleeve and watched all of the skin from my wrist and arm up past my elbow slide down my arm, filling my left hand full of the scalded hot skin in less than five seconds after it happened….. my very first thought was, 'Now I know why Mothers and

Grandmothers get so hysterical when young children go near a pot of boiling water!'

My next thought was of excruciating pain….. I clenched my left hand into a fist to try and do something about the pain. As I tightened the arm muscles, my arm produced large drops of blood that looked like my arm was sweating blood drops.

I thought about what is written about the agony that Jesus went through even *before* He died on the cross, even in prayer looking forward towards completing his mission and that it was so intense that it is written 'He Sweat as it were, Great drops of blood'……

I could hardly take it in that He would willingly choose to go through that kind of pain and agony for me, to redeem and restore me to a relationship with my God and Creator.

I ended up driving myself to the Doctor using only my right hand to drive and shift. During that drive to the emergency room, I started to sing hymns that I knew that focused on the suffering that Jesus endured for me on my behalf, and surprisingly it seemed that nearly '99%' of my pain disappeared for as long as I was singing those hymns, and tears ran down my face as I thought about his great Love for me.

Focus on understanding His love and the reason for His suffering for you on your behalf, and ask yourself, "If this is true, Why would he choose to do this for me?" Understanding any portion of the depth of His love for us can bring tears of appreciation and joyfulness that can wash away fear or pain in your heart.'

Hope Is To Expect Things To Get Better

5th of July 1:55 AM…..Early morning and still awake…. thinking…….. Pastor Jim gave me Hope,…. The darkness shall turn to light….. Sadness shall turn to joy….. Sometimes I can find joy in the midst of sorrow, when I look for it. Sometimes I think there is no 'Wrong Way/Right Way' to look at some of our life situations,……. just a different way.

5th July No one can take your hope away unless you let them. Love is life, and to live life,….. To live is to Love and to Love is to truly live. ….Hope holds life together with Love.

6 July 9 AM Thinking again of one of the greatest experiences of unconditional love I have ever known and experienced was when I sat

and listened to the court worker read the charges on the restraining order. I knew what the truth was, and yet I knew that Alicia believed these misunderstandings and accusations to be true.

Thinking back now to sitting in court listening them read her accusations, when my thoughts went to my Lord Jesus and how he sat quietly listening to the accusations read against him, and he said not a word even though he could prove his innocence.

I remember looking at my '*Kjearest Alicia*' sitting over there and just loving her more and more and more. I could feel nothing other than Love for her, only Love and compassion. And so in seeing her sitting there, I believe that I felt similar to what our Savior did, or at least a greater understanding of his feelings, as they railed against him and he could only Love them with a greater Love. His forgiving spirit was magnified for them and he held nothing against them.

.... I kept thinking then and again now about the evidence of how much Joseph must have Loved Mary,........displayed in his Actions,.... '*and Joseph resolved to divorce her quietly, not willing to make her a public example.*'

9:45 AM waiting on God's will and timing is becoming easier and more peaceful. I am more confident that my original understanding of his will is going to happen and I have a bit of anxious excitement at the same time.

And if I misunderstood somehow, then what is his plan?........ I must wait and see. I believe he has greater joy in store for me than I could possibly dream of, and if sorrow and loneliness is my lot, then I shall be drawn closer to him and his suffering, and this too shall only be an '*Øyeblikk*' (a moment, an 'eye blink') in the realm of eternity.

And then for sure I shall be with my beloved Alicia forever together in the presence of the Trinity, and even so as we began from the first moment as one in spirit and purpose....Shall we be together one day to come in the future??... :>) ....maybe?... or not ..... or what?? .... I can only wait and see.

Learning To Be Patient

10:26 AM, Thinking of Alicia, '*Jeg lengt etter deg*' ..(I long for you (her presence)). .... No tears, no broken heart, just a longing to be with her, and thankful for the joyfulness in the understanding I have been given in the past days and weeks as I am writing down my thoughts and feelings.

......I have a greater appreciation for the Love our Lord has for us, ...and so quietly he waits for us in everything, both in salvation, and our obedience, ... He patiently waits for us to find both.

10:39 AM It would seem to me that Alicia would have to 'test' others the same as my Love for her has been tested, for her to know in her heart if another loves her as much as I do, and if they would willing wait for her as long as I have, or as long as I am willing to wait into the future, of which right now, I just do not know how long that may be,......or may not be..........

10:43 AM It seems that everything I am learning now about the gentle patience and love of the Lord Jesus, I have learned from and because of my love for Alicia. No matter what she has done or I have done, the love only continues to multiply the manifestation thereof.

Unconditional love..... What more can we say than that. Unconditional, no strings attached, just an outpouring of love and, ... how much more perfect is His Love than mine.

12:30 PM I'm eating my lunch and the song on the radio makes me think of Alicia, even though I'm already thinking of Alicia. It seems to me now that every song was '*written about Alicia and for Alicia,*'...... at least as far as I am concerned.

We all have at least one special song that causes us to think of a special someone. Sometimes a song reminds us of someone that was special to us in the past, even though that is not the present situation.

That is still true for me in that when I hear some certain song from the past, for a moment I sometimes am mindful of someone special in my life before now, and those thoughts are quickly set aside to the present moment because now it is only Alicia, completely Alicia for me in my heart, and every moment in my thoughts now is all about my cherished Alicia. Vente, vente, (wait, wait) ... still, my heart is still.

12:35 PM I am in love, and just thinking, waiting, enjoying the feeling of being in love, nothing will ever change away from that. I will always Love her, and Esteem her, with her or without her.

I will always appreciate what she has given to me, with the understanding I have gained in my heart because of knowing her. I am content, and still in my heart. Two words best express my contentment, the Japanese word Satori, and the Norwegian word Fornøyd.

12:45 PM I'm sitting out on the balcony enjoying the pleasantness of the day with a cup of coffee in my hand. I'm looking forward to the day that I can be with Alicia again, if that is possible. I'm just enjoying that thought and holding onto it.

About 80% of the sky is cloudy and Alicia could make every day *'Kjempefint,'*('CjHem pa Fint"Really Great') .....rain or shine her presence would make the day perfect.

12:50 PM The simplicity of the forest, together with it's beauty or the grandeur of the castle experience would be equally the same for me when Alicia is a part of it.

And likewise for me, with our Lord in heaven, whether we are on our knees, in a castle, a church, or walking on the forest path, the moments are all precious for me in the presence of the Lord in the communication of the heart with Him.

2:50 PM Hope,..... Pastor Jim signing his letter *'Respectfully'.....* He has given me a measure of hope.

Hope.... 260 days,... August ?...?......does this actually mean something?? ...or is this just something given to me to give me enough hope to help me survive this present situation??........ When might it be possible that Alicia will first contact me and we will have the chance to be back together with our relationship at some level.

Back together, ...whenever that is possible is first and most important, at least as good friends, and Hopefully, ... I am the *most hopeful* that we will be partners for life, and that I will be the best husband possible because of my experiences now.

3:10 PM Alicia, to me, is a picture of us to our Lord Jesus. He loves us unconditionally. ... He loves us more, far more that I am able to love Alicia and He looks at us as perfect in his sight through himself.

3:18 PM What sorrows Jesus is that we will not come to him, no matter what we have done. He wants our fellowship and all has been forgiven in advance the moment we accept (trust/'believe that it is true') his gift of forgiveness. He desires that communication in prayer and closeness with us.

3:20 PM Our past rejection of him, is the only thing that separates us from him.

3:23 PM.... Love, life, and hope, ... my hope is for the present .....
For Kristie it is much different, she has a certain hope of restoration to her Husband and Daughter in the future.

.... At least I have the hope,... of a chance of restoration to Alicia in this present physical life, and a certain hope of restoration in the future in Heaven. ..... I truly hope that I do not have to wait that long.

For Love?... Or Money?... Or?...

3:57 PM A FB post said, 'Why do people post things that they do??' ....

'Why?' ...... Do they think they are being clever?, ...Who benefits from what they write?, ...Why do people post some of the things they do,???? For their own satisfaction of venting their feelings?? .... or a well thought out post written to encourage others?....

Do we selfishly ask for things for ourselves in prayer? or do we ask God in prayer for things for other peoples' benefit? .... Even if they, or no one else knows that we devoted time in prayer asking for God's Blessings to be poured out upon them.

5:18 PM...................... I do not know if, or when I may come to a point that I might choose not to have Alicia back together with me because, if it were only because of money, it would be an insult to my genuine love for her. ...... Likewise, we cannot purchase for donations of money to a church what God has given us in love for free, ... it is an insult to God for anyone to think that they can 'purchase' a ticket to heaven.

The Old Man And The Missionary

I remember a story told about a missionary that was retiring and moving back to the states. One older man in the community was sad to see him leave even though he had never come to fully understand the message of love and forgiveness he had heard for so many years.

As a parting gift to the missionary the old man presented him with a very large pearl that he had kept for many years. His only son had found the pearl diving, but had stayed down to long and ended up dying because of it.

The missionary realized that the pearl was worth a lot of money, and said that he didn't feel that he should take such a valuable gift from the man because he should have the money to live on himself. He offered to pay him for the value of the pearl, knowing the man needed the money.

The old man said *"You can never pay me enough money for this pearl.* This pearl cost my only son everything in losing his life, you can only accept it as a gift from me for free."

With those words the missionary saw his opportunity to explain to the old man that Salvation could never be bought, because it cost God everything with Jesus taking the old man's place on the cross. It could never be bought, *only accepted as a gift for free.* He then understood.

Love cannot be lukewarm, it must be passionate and burn with compassion, .. And be compassionate, and burn with passion.

Money is nice, and useful, and necessary to a given extent. Yet........ There are some things that money can never buy. Money can buy you 'friends', as long as your money holds out, but it will never buy you a friend who will risk and even lay down his life to save yours because he loves you more than he loves his own life.

Money can build a beautiful church building and pay for a seat for you to sit down in, but it will never buy you a Savior who has laid down his life for you to pay for a place for you in Heaven.

You and I both want a love and a partner in life that chooses to be with us even if we have little money and feels that they have more fullness in life than a multimillionaire, or that we are multimillionaires and we would give it all up in a blink of an eye if that were the only way we could be with that one special person.

Good Health And Happiness Is Wealth

Physical Health,...and Spiritual Health...... Each of these to an extent, are relative to and depend on the health of the other.

A FB friend posted, 'Go for someone who is not only proud to have you but will take every risk just to be with you.'

I thought about this with my feelings for Alicia and I commented, 'Absolutely (my Friend), I am glad for you that you have gained that perspective in life and in a relationship. You only sometimes find out how deep the commitment is after you or they have been through the fire and as the Bible says, Only the gold will remain. And it is worth waiting for, to find this one person, whom no other can replace them and if, or should I say, when, you find that person and you discover that if you might for any reason be apart from them for a while, you will know that it is worth waiting for them, no matter what you choose to give up to have that chance again.'

Sue's FB Post 'People can easily become complacent with a comfortable life until one day they wake up and it is gone' .... This one hit home with me........ Hard.

The Human Brain

Another FB post: 'The human brain starts working the moment we are born and never stops until you stand up to speak in public.' (This post was of course meant to be comical, and sadly there is a little truth to the latter part of it, especially when you consider the things that come out of some people's mouths when they do speak.)

I replied with this comment on her post: "I heard on a radio program some years ago that the brain is functional very near the start of conception and that the child can hear in the latter months through the mother's stomach and it registers in the subconscious brain of the child.

It was the conclusion that possibly, that may be the explanation for the contented and happy child. A child whose arrival was looked forward to with joy and happiness, and that this child was already programmed in their subconscious to the expectation of a happy life. As they consciously learn the language, the conscious brain confirms to the unconscious/subconscious brain the same message of love and happiness in the meanings of the words they now learn.

And likewise the child that was unplanned, unexpected and possibly unwanted was also programmed in the subconscious as an unwelcome addition to the family. Could this explain the children that grow up to be so different, difficult and challenging to work with for parents, teachers, law enforcement employee's etc?.......... Something to think about........."

We should always be able to stand up at a moment's notice and talk about or embrace the things, subjects, beliefs and people we are passionate about.

Karen's FB post: 'It all starts with an idea'

My comment: "Everything begins with thought, everything, absolutely everything. Whether it be a house, car, large factory, the design of a coffee cup or a friendship.

Even a man in prison for robbing a bank, would **not** be there if he **never** *had the* **thought** *or* **idea** that he could rob a bank and get some money.

Thought requires action. First perhaps to write it down on paper which makes it no longer just thought and converts it into something that can be seen, touched and held. Then the thought or idea can be refined, redesigned and made into a solid plan of action that a carpenter can follow to build a house for example. Turn your thoughts into written plans that will help you to take action in the direction of those things, to achieve what you want from your life."

The Tractor Manual And The Rulebook Of Life

Sandy's Facebook post: 'Freedom post: Following the rule book of life/Bible'

My comment: "The 'rulebook of life' reminded me of a story told to me 20 years ago by my friend Kelly from Bucklin Kansas. Kelly said that his Father, when he sold a new John Deere tractor, at delivery would give the farmer the Tractor Owner's Manual and a Bible telling him *'Here's the operators manual for the tractor and the operators manual for the operator'*"

I had the privilege to meet his father Ken one day driving through Kansas on my way to Phoenix to visit my sister Barb and her family. I stop at tractor dealerships in every state as I travel with the same excitement and curiosity that some people have for garage sales!

It was only to be a 10-15 minute stop at a John Deere Dealer in 'Wheat Country' that resulted in Ken greeting me as I came in the door, and a few minute road trip break, turned into a hour long visit with a new friend.

Kelly's Father was such a nice man that I began stopping in to visit him every time I passed through Bucklin on my trips back and forth from Wisconsin to Arizona.

In visiting with Kelly one day in his office after his Father had passed away, Kelly told me about the Tractor Manual/Bible story. I thought to myself, *'That's why he was such a nice man.'*

We should all live our lives toward others that our *'Actions Speak Louder than our Words'* regarding our beliefs and helping people.

Kindness and politeness toward strangers may be the seed planted in their hearts that multiplies itself over and over again to a multitude of strangers that we will never have the opportunity to meet. Each respective manual can keep the Tractor and Man operating smoothly.

Sandy's post for 6 July. "Freedom is not free…. It cost him everything and He gave it all for the one He Loved……… You." ……. Nothing to add to that statement.

The Use And Effect Of Our Power

10:00 PM Tuesday, July 6. Climbing a mountain for me is like waiting for Alicia, you know what is at the top. Just keep going, stop and rest a bit……. And just keep going. …...

There is a HUGE black worm crawling across my path up the mountain. I almost stepped on him with my right foot and I jumped over to miss him….. I could've stepped on him and squashed him…. I have the power over his life, and I also have the power to show mercy and spare him………...

10:10 PM Power must be used carefully…… With great power comes a greater responsibility…..Words have power.

We must always use the power of our words towards others both carefully and wisely. How a person uses power, and for what, Defines, and Reveals who we really are at heart.

10:21 PM We cannot ask God to remove the sin from our life, we must remove ourselves from the sin, or we would be robots. God created us and gave us a free will to choose to love him or not. He says he has forgiven us for all of our sins, Past, Present and 'Future sins in advance' the moment we trust Jesus as our Savior.

For whatever reason, that I do not fully understand, Alicia removed herself from me. ……..what happened?????....

I am now beginning to really believe that God *purposely separated* Alicia and me, to give me a greater and deeper understanding of his Love for all people through *experiencing the deeper understanding of my Love for Alicia.*

Footprints

10:25 PM We are like deer on the path, you can see their footprints. Every step I take carries an impact on the ground, on nature, and on my life, as well as the lives of others around me.

10:37 PM I am walking up on the path to the top of Vettafjell, on the Tingvollfjord side of the mountain. It is the path Alicia and I walked during her February visit.

I am about 50 meters up on the correct path, or I should simply say the most commonly traveled path, because any and all paths are the right path for the most devoted and disciplined mountain climbers. I can now see where I made my mistake when Alicia and I walked up in the snow, over and under the mess of downed tree tops on the steepest part of the mountainside.

I took what looked like the easy path on the forest logging road. What looked like the easiest way to begin with, turned out to be the most difficult in the waist deep snow. Our footprints in the deep snow amongst the tree tops were evidence of my mistake.

I simply was not familiar enough with the mountain to know exactly where I should go that day.

I must think about the easy or more difficult paths I walk in life and the short term/long term benefits or consequences of those choices.

10: 40 PM There is absolute beauty along the way if you look for it. I just noticed some small yellow and orange flowers one quarter to one half inch in size. Even the weeds, …..every plant has its own beauty.

10:42 PM I am one half of the way up on the right path. Alicia and I were a few hundred feet farther over to the left side of this path, where there still lays the mess of down tangled treetops that we had to crawl over in the snow compared to the good path on the same hill, with the same distance up the mountain and 10 times more difficult on that parallel path through and over the tree limbs.

It is the same with our walk in life isn't it. We can choose what looks like an easy path, and most often we do not choose to walk a difficult path, we just find ourselves on it after it's too late to turn back.

From the point on the road where I should've taken to the right and straight up over the hill and then to the left the rest of the way to the mountain top, I continued up the easy mountain road used for logging until

I was at the steepest point to go straight up over the hill to the mountain peak.

It was not until Alicia and I were climbing between and over the down treetops, that I knew we, (.. I, ..) had taken the wrong way….. It was too late to change anything then, we just had to continue the path we were on. It was a good lesson learned, without serious consequences……..*but,* Alicia had to suffer the consequences of my mistake.

Usually only we suffer the consequences of our personal mistakes in life. Sometimes our partner in life, and even our family or friends suffer heartaches because of our choices. 'No man is an Island,' every action creates a reaction. It is usually good to 'think' before we speak, or act.

My Rainbow

10:45 PM… There is a double rainbow over the fjord. It is so near to me on this side of the fjord that I can see where it touches the ground a just a few meters away from me. It's very presence mesmerizes me……..I recalled the old Irish saying that there is a pot of gold at the end of the rainbow. I did not go and look for it.

…………..I have never experienced this before!…. I did not think it was even possible to be so close to the end of the rainbow……I know that the sunlight is reflected because of the water in the air……But while I don't fully understand it, I certainly am enjoying it!

10:47 PM…. There is a stone path here in the forest. People have laid out flat stones to step on in this soft area nearly at the top of the mountain. Sometimes the stones are close enough that there is a stone for each step, but even when they are further apart it is clear which direction you should take. There are enough stones that you can easily see from one stone to the next,…. Then you know you are following the correct path. Those steppingstones were covered with snow when Alicia and I first climbed the mountain together. …………..

WOW!…. It is like I am in the left side of a huge rainbow, standing alone!!! I was fascinated to just be so close to the end of the rainbow only a few minutes ago, and now it has engulfed me with *color all around me*!!!!!!

I thought that this was supposed to be impossible to happen,……….To actually be standing *IN* the rainbow ….. I cannot understand this…………. this must be *a once in a lifetime experience!!*

10:52 PM. The rainbow is just *huge* and it reaches to the Heavens, where the promise comes from. The second side is over the top of the fjell.

11:00 PM. The very first rainbow that is spoken of was the one Noah saw. …. I'm just thinking that since it is said that the first rainbow was placed as a promise, it must've been a combination of shock and awe for Noah to behold it. ……I think I can understand a bit of that experience, *from my experience right now!*

6 Degrees Of Separation

July 7th 12:25 AM………..It is said that there is 6 degrees of separation between most people on earth, who can bring strangers together through the friend, of a friend, of a friend.

As I understand it my friend Marshall is friends with Sir Richard Branson, so it would be because of that, I believe that one day I may have the opportunity to shake hands with Sir Richard Branson. If that happens, it will likely be because of Marshall that I shall have that privilege.

Will it be because of? ….. Perhaps, Pastor Jim that Alicia and I will be reunited??…. Will it be because of us as Christians, that our friends are introduced to Jesus? ………. the biggest question in that is, …… Is there anything about us and our Actions (not just our words,) towards our friends and strangers that would make them have any desire to know Jesus?

Or, ….. would it sadly be that because of the Words we speak, and our Actions Supporting,… or *Contradicting* what we say, that would cause them to not want anything to do with Jesus, …because of us?? …. That indeed would be tragic. ……………………….. We have an important job.

12:48 AM I'm finished with writing the postcards I wish to send. Just sitting here looking out the window of the cabin beholding everything I see in nature, thinking about the wisdom of God, and creation, …… How does everything hold together????????

12:55 AM. Singing these words to the melody of a song in my thoughts;
Have I told you how much I love you, Have I told you how much I care.
Have I told you how much I want to share, the rest of my life with you.
Have I told you how much I love you,
Let me show you instead of tell you.

Our Lives Should Demonstrate His Love

Some of my friends here cannot understand how I can meet someone on the train up from Oslo, find out the woman is a Christian, lives half an hour drive from where I live here in Norway, and on the following Sunday be invited to have dinner with her and her husband, and their three children.

It is our love for him, who first loved us and gave himself for us, that fills our heart with love for both those who have seen that Jesus took their place on the cross, and especially those who have not yet to see and understand how much Jesus loves each and every person. Our lives should show his love and not just tell it.

…….. It is early-morning, I'm not sure what time it is, …….. Just thinking, that it may not go the full two years and perhaps within that time, Alicia will choose to be back together with me.

Before some point in time I believe she will choose to be back together with me, …or she may never be back together with me, for her own reasons, unknown to me, … or is it possible that she may wait too long, and I may be on a different path or commitment, on which I cannot turn around………..

I will provide for Alicia either way as I am able, regardless of which path of personal relationship I choose to walk.

July 7 11:47 AM Everything in life is about hope and hope adds everything to life. It is like the woman in the brown dress at the La Crosse airport ……. It is not important whether someone is tall or short, slender or not so slender, etc. It is only important to experience the emotion and connection of that look in the eye … that says more than words can tell.

12:08 PM One foolish word or action can destroy a life, yours or that of another person,…… One wise word or action can change your life or another's forever for good.

12:12 PM It is not that Alicia is the only one to bring me happiness, it is that I desire to give to her more than for myself. I sincerely believe that I will give her more devotion as a husband than anyone, or possibly more than everyone she has ever known in her life all put together could, or would.

12:45 PM I am next to Karihavet and I am noticing a very unusual disturbing of the water. It is as if the wind is causing only a small portion of the water to move, it reminds me of what is written that the spirit moved upon the waters.

Whatever it is I can definitely see the effect of it in the moving of the water in the midst of the still water all around it.

We also can see the effect of the moving of the Spirit in our lives, ... And..... do others see that affect in our lives for good for both ourselves and others .... I wonder what others would say about me regarding that?

It is written, *'Come beside the still waters.'* I am enjoying the peacefulness, quietness and time to ponder my thoughts here by the water .... the still water.

The Undelivered Message

1:37 PM How long does something or someone wait?? There has to come a time when it is no longer an option for one reason or another. The spring planting season only waits so long before it becomes too late to plant a crop in time for it to mature into food before the winter comes.

I remember a story regarding this told in a Sunday school class when I was maybe around 14 or 16 years old.

A woman of retirement age had lost her husband and later as she prepared to sell their home and move to a new dwelling place she cleaned out the entire home of personal belongings.

The home she and her husband had lived in was actually the same home she grew up in, together with her parents and siblings.

As she went through the things in the attic, she came across a brown leather jacket that had belonged to her 10-year-old brother at the time she was of college age.

She had a serious relationship then with a wonderful young man and they had been headed toward marriage. They had a disagreement about something and she had told the young man that she never wanted to see him again. Brokenhearted the young man left.

They lived some distance apart and the young woman regretting the break-up, wrote a long letter of apology and asked if they could get together and talk again. She ended the letter with a sentence that if he was not interested in talking to her again she would understand, and no reply would be necessary.

She gave the letter to her younger brother to take to the post office. She waited and waited and his answer never came.

As she took up her brothers coat in her hands she quickly went through the pockets to see if there was anything in them, and she found a letter, her letter, to the young man she loved. She never received a reply from him because he had never received her letter.

She sat there with the letter in her hand and read the words she had written him. She thought about her life, she had lived a good life, and had a good husband whom she had recently lost ….…...But, she could not help but wonder how her life may have been different if her letter had reached the young man she was in love with.

A few words fittingly spoken can change the direction of our lives forever. Her message of love and asking for forgiveness never reached the one she had loved.

Do we listen to the message of Love God has for us?…. While we still have time to receive it into our hearts?

Love Supports Hope

4:45 PM I know that God can restore all things the first time, every time. Treat every time that you are with someone you care about as if it is the first time you are with them, such as the first time you hold your child or the first moment that you know you have met the love of your life, and every time you are with them, value your time with them as if you knew it were your last time. Do this in all things.

6:49 PM I am sitting in the middle of friends, and yet I am sorrowful in my heart as I think of my Kjærest. Enduring the pain after the loss, reality comes back and hits you hard when you are not looking.

7:53 PM Life can sure change in a year. All the hours' long phone conversations each day with Alicia while I was in Norway and she was back home in Minnesota.

…… Jeremy and Izzy,… for Kristie and all of their family, a part of each other's lives every single day, until one day, ….. gone forever from this physical life.

Hope is eternal,…and,… How does one deal with loss. It is the same, …or I probably should say at least similar for me losing Alicia and Marc out of my life for me, as it is for them …only I know it is much worse for Kristie and her family. Seeing them in Heaven will be wonderful, and it does nothing to fill the emptiness here now.

10:30 PM Being without Alicia in my life after she became a part of my life, is like my spiritual relationship to the Lord. Once I came to know my Savior the night of my 23rd birthday, I can't imagine what it would be like to lose that daily communication with Him.

Life without Alicia is empty, after coming to know her. There's nothing more to seek after. Others that are pretty, social status, nothing matters. There's only one person, one heart, and one that can look me in the eye like she does.

Once you have met the Savior it is the same thing, there is not the same satisfaction in the things that were before. My perspective was completely, wonderfully and excitedly different about everything, from that night forward.

July 8 9:15 AM I have an absolute hope, and absolutely no hope at the same time. ….. It is the same thing and yet different. …….. Jeremy and Kristie ………hope gone forever here in this life.

I do not want to address 'no hope' because that would be to give up hope…..

…….That is *Hope*, to NEver accept that there is no hope….. Again I do not think it will go two years, ……but I don't know for certain what God's plan and purpose is for both, or either Alicia and me.

Just pondering my thoughts,… I want to believe Alicia may one day choose to be back together with me, perhaps before two years go by???... maybe it will take longer…. or never? I must just wait and see, and I know that she is worth the wait whatever it 'costs' me to wait and find out.

'Conditional' And 'Unconditional Love'

July 8 5:21 PM Where do all these thoughts come from? ….Why so many now, ….Am I now listening to the Lord? What moves our heart to give someone another chance,… or for them to give us another chance?

We have all probably at least once said or heard someone say *"They deserve another chance."* Sometimes someone may have said that *"They HAd their chance,* and now they must suffer the consequences."

At some point in some peoples individual lives they ran out of chances, be it personal, business, or their responsibility to society and they must now suffer the consequences whatever the cost.

A person in a relationship (personal or business) that made a mistake or offended the other person may well deserve another chance to get it right or make things right in most circumstances. Often these relationships, and/or friendships become stronger in the long run, when issues are resolved and a greater respect is born between the two persons involved.

An employee that made a big and/or costly mistake for a business because of an obvious lack of experience or ability may or may not merit another chance based on the company's owner or manager's assessment of the risk involved to the good of the company.

The victim of abuse in a personal relationship, married or any other, may well have no obligation to the abuser to give them another chance, even if children are involved and maybe especially if children are involved.

In either case business or personal, it is a personal choice on the part of the boss or the victim to give someone a second chance.

The decision of the boss to give another chance would likely be based on the possible future benefit to the company that would be greater than the initial cost of that person's mistake. Sometimes a boss may personally know the person or be aware of someone's personal situation or predicament and be simply moved with compassion to help them by giving them another chance.

Likely almost always it would be a spirit of unconditional love, compassion and forgiveness that would move the heart of a victim of abuse or some other great personal offence to give someone a second .... or more chances.

It is the *undeserved chances* that fall into the *unconditional love* perspective for us as humans.

The greatest of these is God's Love and Compassion to us to give us another chance, even though we do not deserve it.

6:05 PM Alicia can always call me, and at the snap of a finger I will be back, I have no need to ask any questions, I need no explanations, just to be back together, as if nothing had ever went wrong. There is no trial period necessary for me on my part, just a yearning to be back together if that is possible.

That is the power of unconditional love, it always seeks restoration, it always gives love and hope every possible chance in our life. The far greater unconditional Love that Jesus has for us led him to the cross in our place, on our behalf. Jesus restored my relationship to himself as if I had *never* did anything wrong. Jesus asked me no questions, asked for no explanations, he just offered me unconditional restoration between me and himself as my creator.

Forgiveness... *For*-giveness

'*For*-giveness' is a unique Norwegian view of the word forgiveness by Anna Marie (Lisa), my friend Mortens Mother. It was used in its 'hyphenated' form by the Pastor giving the sermon at Lisa's funeral.

The Pastor explained that while visiting with Lisa at Bethel Home, where she lived the last chapter of her life, she had clarified to him that forgiveness was '*For*-giveness,' ('before-giveness' or 'advance-giveness.')

To say 'Thanks-in-advance' when Lisa would ask me to do some favor or small job for her, she would tell me 'Forhånd Takk' ('before-hand thanks' (or 'thanks in advance' as we would say in English)) before I had even started the job.

While I was well aware of the full meaning and use of 'Forhånd Takk,' I had missed the emphasis and significance Lisa put on the word '*For*-giveness' in our conversations over the years on forgiveness and salvation. She saw the significance of the word '*for*' within the English word forgiveness, because of the frequent use of the word '*for*' in front of many Norwegian words.

As I sat with the Church congregation on the day of her funeral, I remembered the tone and emphasis of Lisa's voice in our conversations as she always said the word *for*giveness.

I had overlooked the significance of her emphasis on the word *For*(giveness) thinking that it was just her Norwegian accent and way of speaking Norwegian words carrying over into her speaking of English words.

The *moment* I heard the Pastor say that Lisa had said to him that forgiveness was **FOR**-giveness, I remembered our many conversations together, hearing her put emphasize on '*for*giveness.' That was likely the main reason that Lisa had such a content, easy going personality and that she lived with that forgiving spirit of kindness towards all people. Truly, all were welcome at Lisa's home for coffee. Actions speak louder than words, and Lisa lived that way. She will be missed, blended together with many fond memories.

Wildman Cat

There is one more story that I must tell about Lisa's kindness and compassion that she showed to animals as well as people. Lisa was always concerned that the goats, cows and horses on the farm had plenty of hay to eat in winter and if the pasture grass was short during summer dry weather. She also always had food outside the back door of the house on a tray for the dogs and cats on the farm.

One day while I was working in the shop in the big machine shed at the farm, Lisa came out to the shed carrying a bowl of cat food looking for her 'Wildman Cat.'

She said that a new cat had showed up at the farm and he lived in the shed because he was too scared to come to the house. She named him Wildman Cat because she couldn't catch him, and she brought food out to the shed so she was sure he would have something to eat each day.

One day I bought a wagon load of hay bales from Mort that he had parked in the shed. I just hooked up the wagon to my pickup truck and pulled it the 15 miles home to my farm and parked it in my shed for a few days before I unloaded it into the dairy barn hay loft so I could take Mortens wagon back to him.

When I was about half done unloading the hay, I picked up one bale and a cat jumped out of a hole between the bales and dove into another hole between two other bales. After this game of hide and seek happened a couple more times, I caught a good glimpse of the cat and saw that it was not one of the cats from my farm. I thought that it must be Lisa's 'Wildman Cat.'

Knowing that catching a wild farm cat was both difficult and potentially 'dangerous,' I went to the shop and got a pair of thick leather welding gloves that extended halfway up to my elbows so I could hang onto Wildman Cat, if I could catch him.

I had another person helping me that day so he picked up one bale at a time until I saw Wildman Cat hiding in a hole and I grabbed him before he knew what was happening. I was *REally* happy I was wearing the welding gloves because holding on to Wildman Cat was like trying to hang on to the 'Tasmanian Devil.'

I put Wildman Cat in the Ford extended cab pickup and he immediately jumped into the back seat and hid while I drove him back home to Lisa's farm. I left him in the truck when I went to the house to tell Lisa the story and that I had brought Wildman Cat back home. I backed the truck into the shed and Lisa was so happy when she saw Wildman jump out of the truck!

It was the most enthusiastic, sincere and biggest thank you I ever got from Lisa as she said *'Tusen, Tusen Takk'* (Thousand, Thousand Thanks) over and over again for bringing her Wildman Cat home. She said that she had been worried all week about what had happened to her Wildman Cat when he didn't show up for his cat food each day.

Lisa's concern for Wildman Cat was further evidence of her concern and compassion for every living thing.

We should all live in a way that our actions leave a legacy of good for others to remember.

God *for*gives us in salvation in that Jesus died for us, *providing* eternal *for*giveness for all of the sins we would ever commit in our *entire* life even *before* we were born,… *applying* this *for*giveness to our account the *moment* we trust his word that Jesus has *paid* the debt and *consequences* of our sins against God in full.

God *for*gives us when we ask on a *daily* basis for our many human failures towards both himself and our offences towards other people, in *addition* to our one time *permanent forgiveness for our eternal security.*

The *daily* forgiveness God gives us keeps or maintains our *daily communication* with him, similar to simple *apologies* between a husband and wife, or between two friends that *maintains* a happy, harmonious relationship.

Trust

July 8, 9:09 PM I am looking at a Krifast 'brevkort' (postcard) with pictures of the Krisfast High Suspension Bridge, the Krifast floating bridge and the Krifast tunnel under the sea.

(The fascinating Krifast system includes the Gjemnessundbrua, the Bergsøysundbrua and the Freifjordtunnelen under the fjord.)

We couldn't go without them, and we trust them to take us safely across. ..... How many people, who or what do we put our trust in emotionally, physically? or spiritually?

The Power In Prayer And Words

A thought came to me on Prayer, ... *Never underestimate the power of a woman in prayer, and motivation.* ....God has given them something special that I do not yet fully understand.

...... I just know that they have some greater measure of something than we men do. .... It is enough for me now to simply know that there is some special difference between us men and women, and to respect it.

10:00 PM Too many Christians have clammed up into tight little religious groups that pat each other on the back saying "Praise the Lord Brother" and use a lot of churchy language that makes them feel good and those around them and,....... maybe it makes Christianity look artificial to nonbelievers,........ destroying any hope of reaching them.

Many others like to say feel-good things and pat each other on the back likewise. Not too many of us, myself included like to hear rebuke and sometimes we need to hear it.

First it should come from the Lord if we are in tune listening to what the Spirit is saying, which will come first as guidance, gently and lovingly. If we ignore that, it will become more stern in the Lords loving, chastening guidance.

Only if we continue to ignore the Lords pleading with us, He may use another brother, or even the unsaved to rebuke and chasten us.

Some years ago I came into a small country store, where several farmers had gathered for coffee. I was well acquainted with the most of them and good friends with three of them.

I do not know what they were talking about when I came in, and one of my good friends jokingly said "And here comes the worst one of the bunch."

My sin came upon my heart, and his words cut my heart in two. His words cut more deeply than any preacher from the pulpit ever could have. God simply used my friend's mouth to speak his word to me.

10:25 PM There are pictures of trains in a magazine from many places in the world, ...are you on tour, ...on track in your life?......... Or just wandering around in life as if you are in the forest,…. lost? …….You must have some path of understanding and consistency in your life to know that you are on track to get to where you want to be.

10:46 PM Word book in Norwegian/English. ….Words are just words, and mean only what we attach them to, we make a word represent a thing, and the same words can mean entirely different things in different languages.

A common word in one language may be inappropriate to use in another language, having an entirely different meaning to it. Sometimes we lose the meaning of the word by idle overuse of it. ……

'Awesome' for example; It's meaning has been watered down from the intense magnitude it was intended to imply.

Learning to speak Norwegian has given me an entirely new perspective on my choice of what words to use, both in speaking, and now in writing to clearly convey the importance of a message. …….. And I have learned that sometimes, …… saying less, says more.

The Importance Of Communication:
Written, Verbal And Prayer

(Postcard to Pastor Jim) *Dear Pastor Jim, I bought a few postcards today and tonight I went up on the mountain top, to sign my name in the book there and went over to Ola's cabin up here where I am now, almost midnight I think. The sun just set about one half hour ago, and it is full light yet. Got your letter when my Mom picked up my mail, I had her open it and read it over the phone. She is forwarding it to me here and I will send from here as FJC. I agree with you and I am comfortable now also. I will share with you what I do that it may be of help in your effort. Thank you so much for the kind reply. Respectfully, Curt*

Ninth of July 1:01 AM Jesus proclaims his love to us like a man or a woman proclaiming their love for each other to friends and to others. Sometimes the intended one that is loved by another does not want to hear it, both in human relationships and God's proclamation of love towards us.

Communication is so important! I believe that this is the reason some people 'Talk to themselves' out loud, if they live alone or seldom have contact with other people. Sometimes people talk to a pet cat, dog or any other animal to fill that need for communication. It is amazing what they can understand.

An Amish farmer once told me that he bought a farm and the previous owner asked him if his old Collie dog could just live out the rest of his life on the only farm he had ever known as home. Aden told me that they were happy to do that for Tom's dog. Aden said that for the first two weeks they thought that dog was the dumbest box of rocks they had ever seen. Then they realized, 'That dog doesn't understand German!'

They started talking to him in English and he obeyed right away. They then spoke both English and German simultaneously for each command and Aden said "The 'Old Dog' learned German in about two weeks!!" ….Yes, 'Old dogs *can* learn new tricks!' Do animals know how to listen better than we do?

The *'Old Dog'* only had to *'listen,'* to learn…. He did not have to 'study German' like a student would. He simply *listened* (with a *desire to learn*!!) to what was being said in relation to what was happening simultaneously to the English word commands.

We likewise have to listen, together with a desire to learn, to improve our human relationship(s). We can also learn to listen when God speaks to our hearts, whether it is through his written word, thoughts that cross our mind or his speaking to every person in the world through the nature, the realm of his creation, including the beauty of the star filled sky above.

God created us to have communication with us. He gave us a free will to reject, or choose to talk with him.

Writing a letter to someone is one way to communicate with someone when we cannot speak with them in person. Hundreds of years ago writing a letter or sending a verbal message through a 'Messenger' person was the only means of communication over many miles of distance. God wrote us a long letter of his Love for us in his written word. We can discover that when we read it. Prayer is another 'Long distance method of communication.'

I am so thankful for Diane and Linda praying for me, and Alicia. I appreciate their kindness toward me, and taking time to pray for both Alicia and me as an individuals, and Alicia and I together, if that should be.

Their actions strengthen my hope. If you have *hope*, you can tolerate, …or a better perspective would be, *endure the unknown and wait for anything.*

Only Half Of The Story

Ninth of July 9 AM……. Thoughts on writing another postcard to Pastor Jim, …….Sometimes we are afraid to say something because we may not be able to say everything, and only half of the story is no story. I know this is what happened between Pastor Jim and me.

Again, it is just like the woman at the well that answered Jesus when he said: go and bring your husband and she answered "I have no husband."(The truth, and only part of the truth) ….. Jesus replied to her, you have answered truthfully, "You have no husband, for you have had five husbands and he who you have now is not your husband."(The whole truth concerning her regarding a husband)

The first Sunday I spoke with Pastor Jim, everything I told him was the truth, ….. and not all of the story at first because I was testing him to see what he believed and how he thought.

I often upon meeting a new person, if the conversation moves into talking about religion or beliefs, I ask them what they believe before I say what I believe, getting their thoughts without my perspective influencing what they may say to me.

I know what I believe and how I think, and it helps me to understand what they believe and what they think to get their own thoughts without the influence of my thoughts.

Alicia asked me a simple question one day, and I told her a simple reply that was the truth, and it was only a small part of the bigger picture and longer story…..

I can see now how she viewed it inaccurately in its incompleteness, and she probably lost some confidence in my abilities.

I had an agreement with one farmer, that one day prevented me from making an agreement with another farmer, the second farmer got really mad that I would not make an agreement with him regarding a potential situation between us, and it severed our friendship for over 10 years.

It came to pass one day that the situation was advantageous for both of us to do business together again.

The whole process went well and a few days into that situation, I said to the second farmer, remember 10 years ago when you got mad that I would not sell you the one extra machine that I had?.... He replied "Yes." "(The first farmer) has long retired and our agreement is no longer in effect, so

I can explain it to you now." I explained to him the agreement I had with the other farmer and why I could not make an agreement with him.

The second farmer replied to me, "You gotta' do what you gotta' do, when you give your word, you gotta' keep it." That full and complete explanation, fully and completely restored our friendship with an even greater respect for each other than what existed before.

Restoration is always sweeter than the original state, because we have the chance to experience the loss, and appreciate more fully the value we had, and now have again. This can apply to business relationships, personal relationships, and restoration on a spiritual level is the absolute best.

Dealing With Loss Through Understanding

10:19 AM The shock of loss keeps hitting me. ...... I think of Kristie, and how the reality of her loss of Jeremy and Izzy must sometimes come back to hit her as if it were all a bad dream, if only it were......, there is no hope for her of them coming back home here to her in this life, and yet I have that absolute hope of the possibility of that happening for me with Alicia and Marc.

I did not just lose a girlfriend....... In my heart, ...I lost my family. Just a year ago Marc called '*The three of us a family*'..... They were the sweetest words I ever heard come out of his mouth to me........... He said so much with so few words, ...

...... yet, in a way I'm almost glad I made the mistake, or mistakes or whatever it was that led to losing my personal relationship with Alicia, because of the blessings of understanding that have come to me this past year.

.........Especially of lately and the thoughts of the Lord Jesus that I have, when he shows me the parallel of my love for Alicia and Marc, and his greater love for me, and all people, so that I have been able to better understand and feel with my heart a deeper comprehension of the depth of his great love for all of mankind.

I am able to acknowledge and better understand the love He feels for all men great and small and how important it is to convey thoughts of the message of salvation to the world in part by the way of my hearts experience and how important one person can be to another.

Pastor Jim, in conveying a negative or positive message about me to Alicia, …….. and that which we convey of our Lord and our love for him to others …………… Is our message negative or positive in the eyes of others????

11:00 AM Sitting alone here on a stump in the forest, I realize that it is good to eat a piece of dry bread once in a while, just to appreciate the steak dinner with fine wine at an eloquent restaurant when it comes. For me it is like being without, or with Alicia.

11:05 AM ……… *Thank You Lord, for giving me Alicia in my life. Thank you for everything she is to me and for everything that you have allowed to happen and for the previous and present understanding to me of my love and devotion to Alicia and Marc and the even greater understanding you have now given me of yourself and your love for me,…… and for each and every other person. And I thank you for giving me hope in Alicia and I, in that what you have established you will fulfill according to your purpose. Thank you for the opportunities before me that I may embrace them fully and use the prosperity thereof not only for myself, but for my family and the drawing of the hearts of all men possible, to you, by every effort. Thank you for all the failures in my life that permit me to be where I am today, and not where I thought I wanted to be some years ago. Amen*

12:22 PM …………..This whole life experience without Alicia in it is very important to my understanding.

A Mouse In The Corner

1:08 PM When you know that people are talking about you, is it just idle gossip, or about something noble or worthwhile? I remember one day back in the 80's when I did a lot of custom harvesting for other farmers, I would frequently eat at Dick's South Lawn, a 24 Hr restaurant in Viroqua before returning home (No cooking, quick to eat and *no dishes to wash!*).

One day as I was eating I heard the people at the table next to me talking about a large farmer that had started harvesting corn already. One man said, "Oh, that's 'Custom Curt' combining that corn for him." Since I was eating and I had my mouth full it took me a minute before I could chew and swallow my food.

As I did this I looked at them while they looked back at me, …… and kept right on talking about me and how I did things! ….. By the time I was able to swallow my food I thought, "They don't have a clue who I am!!!"

It was quite an experience for me to sit like a mouse in the corner and listen to them continuing to talk about my custom work business. I was glad that everything they said was positive. From that experience I realized that I never wanted to say anything about someone that I was not willing to say to their face.

Traveling The Road To Understanding

A Facebook friend posted again, 'There are many paths to God.' ……. I believe there are many paths and situations in life that can bring us to the understanding of the Cross, which is proclaimed to be the door to God. ………..I wonder if the person that posted this, is so uncertain of their destiny that they are hoping this may be true.

…. I think I may have wanted to believe this when I was a teenager, ….. so I could do it 'My way.'

…. I am thankful now, that I understand that I am certain, *'That I know, that I know, what I needed to know.'*

All afternoon I have noticed the seagulls floating carefree in the air, in circles over Kari Havet. It has brought a gentle peacefulness to my heart. It has given me rest for this day.

Saturday, 10 July 3:00 AM………..Lying awake, thinking about how I made myself guilty for her sake. I see her as perfect, …….. and I will say nothing against her.

It is not like I think that I am a goody two shoes or something, I simply have never been upset or angry with Alicia. For example, She could do something that could hurt my feelings perhaps, but I am convinced that I would never be upset and angry with her.

……. It would seem perhaps that I am not speaking in theory, but in this present situation, I am speaking from experience, and what I am experiencing now. I am not angry, or even hurt so to speak,… just sad that I do not have the privilege to be in her presence……. I really truly miss her.

July 10 10:00 AM I have found a perfect love in Alicia, …… nothing has destroyed or diminished it. This morning we are traveling across the fjord to Halsa. We are on tour to the furniture factory store in Todalen.

There is always an excitement every time we go on the road. I have traveled these roads along the fjords so many times I am familiar with and look for many special things in the beauty of my Norwegian homeland.

I am remembering exciting things that have happened throughout my life and the last 20 years or so with travels in both Norway and America, and especially here in Norway last year both before and during when Alicia and Marc came to visit.

I was planning things for us to do here and places to go, excited to share as much as I could with them in the couple weeks of time we had together here.

I remember just being totally focused on just having them here with me. I thought nothing of what would unpredictably come afterwards.

Now, it's just a memory of the exciting days we spent together,…. but the sweet taste is lost. Strawberries will always be strawberries, the taste is always the same, but the satisfaction of the sweetness cannot be fully enjoyed in the emptiness of loneliness.

Without Alicia in my life, all of the happy enjoyable experiences in life for me now are like enjoying the taste of the most delicious strawberry desert you have ever tasted, …….…….at the funeral of your best friend.

We are still on the ferryboat traveling over Halsafjord, having a coffee and Svele, (a unique Norwegian pancake that is eaten cold folded in half, with a sugar and butter cream spread in the middle)…… As much as I love the taste of Svele, I am just not enjoying it today.…

Thinking of Alicia, ….for me nothing in my life now is fully enjoyed without Alicia being some part of it. ………. If I could just enjoy hearing her voice again, …..even if just over the phone.

There is a song on the radio, and instead of enjoying the song, it is just adding to my heartache,…… The words I heard are, "You are so beautiful to me, everything I hope for, everything I need," ………yes,……..more than words can ever tell.

Remembering again, not listening,…….. not LISTENing …… hearing Alicia's words she spoke, and not hearing what she was saying in between the lines.

11:57 AM Bonnie Tyler song on the radio, *Total Eclipse of the Heart* ………..… Yes, I am having a total eclipse of the heart.

We are driving in some new area for me now. Thinking that most people going on a trip enjoy themselves as they see new things, and even though we are driving through some beautiful new area for me, there is just no joy in it for me today without being able to share this experience with Alicia.

Any place is the best with her, regardless of the scenery. .... Her absence leaves a terrible void in the present.

12:22 PM We are at the furniture store. Ola and Martha are looking at some new furniture together, and I remember the times that Alicia and I went shopping for things together, and I was just so content. I was never bored when she wanted to look at things. I just tagged along content to be with her.

There's a waterfall a short distance away in back of the furniture store, Alicia would really enjoy the beauty of this place. All of this beautiful furniture here is important to our lives. It is part of our life to be enjoyed.

For the moment now, I am just standing by the window looking out at the waterfall and stream that runs past the building enjoying the contentment of looking at it.

12:48 PM Just thinking,.......I must write the thoughts of my heart to Pastor Jim about Alicia for my peace of mind.....................

1:00 PM The thundering water fall is about 100 meters back from the store. It is quite a sight in front of me, ... and the noise. The same water that was so powerful in both sight and sound, now flows past me in a small pool near me with barely a ripple. The same tumultuous water is now still, quiet and crystal clear.

There is a large rock of which the water has washed out holes in it. Only the solid stone remains, and as with human love when tested, only the solid love remains. .... With His love, his is the most solid and permanent love, and... He is always there to comfort me.

There is a peaceful area in the forest behind us seemingly more powerful than the noise of the water. The still water joins again the force of the stream, the water swirls and carries away and always comes to rest in the end....... So is life, big or small all comes to rest.

Here some of the water somehow even flows back again from the force, uphill and against the law of gravity, ... Sometimes, we must go against the flow in life..............All of this is so thought provoking.

1:11 PM Life must go on,............. Regardless................... Hold back the river and something will eventually burst.

1:14 PM ...You want enough of the river and the life it possesses, to sustain you and give you life, ...and not so much to be drowned by it, ...and like the still pools of water, some quiet times to just be alone and reflect, ignoring the noise of the waterfall.

1:15 PM Only in the still water can you see the bottom clearly. The rushing white water hides the beauty below.

In the still water pool there are so many unique small stones below the surface where all of it comes to rest after being subjected to the force of the water above the pool.

Like the rushing water, the challenging times in our lives will usually pass by us, leaving us defeated, or polishing us to become stronger and wiser. It is our choice of how we want to see things. It is our perspective that determines the outcome and effect of these things for our future.

1:18 PM There is a magazine of some kind that lay washed up on the bank and all stuck together, not readable, and therefore useless. The water destroyed it because the paper pages have no defense against water...........
How can the things we learn in life be useful to ourselves, ... and to others?

1:20 PM There's a small stone bridge on the path up to the falls, making it easier and safe to go up there. ....I must see what is up there.

1:24 PM I am standing up on the rocks by quite a big waterfall, the water comes down with such force and quickly ends up in the still quiet pool and quickly again it goes from still to a rapid descent to the lower levels.

There's about a 2 foot deep pool that looks safe to walk in, and yet get carried away in this water and at some point the water will destroy you.

There is an iron handle that has been inserted solidly into the stone and you can remain safe as long as you hold tightly to it.........

I am reminded of the similarities in life, like the water, life can be still and quiet and in the blink of an eye it can turn tumultuous, sometimes exciting, and sometimes dangerous. .... Hold fast to a safe anchor physically and spiritually.

1:26 PM I walked out onto the rock in the midst of it and I'm safe on the rock. Some water can splash on me and get me wet but it does not have the power to harm me. I am standing only 2 meters away from the strongest flow. I can observe it safely without any problem from the water's force on the rock.

It is similar to living next to someone going through the challenges of life and we can do little or nothing to help them in that moment.

….. What would, 'I do'/'you do', if we KNew what the day would bring forth for someone?…..

Maybe it is good that we do not know what the future has in store for us physically and emotionally in this life….. and I do know that *it IS important to know* what eternity has in store for us.

Since we usually do not have that exact insight for daily life, we can only be optimistic about life and encourage those around us whenever we can. I have learned that those of us that have experienced the force of the thundering waterfall upon us perhaps have a good viewpoint and advice of how to survive a situation, while someone else is experiencing what we already have gone through.

8:00 PM To be married to someone else than Alicia, …. I could love and be loved, and maybe not be in love the same because your first love is gone. It is the same as a Christian no longer in daily fellowship with Jesus once you have experienced it. Someone can find a measure of happiness for a while and not enjoy that perfect contentment that you once knew. ….. Last year I was 100% content with Alicia a part of my life, so much so that I stopped hoping for more in life, I had found what I was searching for, and now with her absence from my life, I somehow want to give even more to Alicia.

8:49 PM There is no place to go and I cannot go there……. Like each the rich man and Lazarus, neither could go to the other……… I am sitting with friends and I have nothing to say, I am doing less than 1% of the talking….. Quite unusual for me.

Expressing Our Feelings

July 11 – 1:15 AM …. Songs all search for genuine love, and some even touch on it. Sometimes when we have nothing to say,…or don't know what to say, the right song says it all.

This is true for both the Physical and Spiritual aspect of Love. A bashful or 'tongue-tied' boy or girl, man or woman, that perhaps can't find the words to fully express their feelings towards the other, can best express their feelings either while dancing together, giving each other the gentle hugs or a stronger embrace as the words of the song become their own, or simply while walking or sitting together holding hands and the tenderness of their hearts is revealed in the gentleness of the touch of their intertwined fingers listening to the music.

Likewise the expression of Spiritual Love is sometimes best expressed in joyful singing, of both traditional hymns and newer songs.

This is true for me in that many times when I am finished praying about something, I will sing or hum a verse or two of a familiar hymn and sometimes then 'continue praying' by making up words as I go to fit the tune 'singing' a new song in prayer.

It seems that music, blended together with the thoughts and quest for genuine Love, gives us the Hope of finding that Love, Physically in another Person, and Spiritually, at peace with God.

These songs have the greatest meaning and value to our hearts, after we have found each of those quests for love personally.

Sunday July 11 If someone may die of something, a man will pray to a God that he does not believe in to help him....... You *must* have some kind of hope...........even if you are not sure of it.

Breaking Bread On The Mountain

5:52 PM This Sunday afternoon I chose to go on top of the nearest mountain, Vattefjell, to break bread, and to be alone to pray. I chose to go up and spend an hour or so from 4 pm until 5 pm Norwegian time.

Since we are seven hours ahead of Central Time in America, at the very same moment, Pastor Jim was holding the 9:00 am church service, where Alicia attended.

For the first 15-20 minutes I sang hymns while Alicia would have been singing with the congregation.

For the next half hour I prayed for Pastor Jim and the message he had chosen to speak on, and that God would add his blessing to the message to each person listening to it.

For the last 10 minutes of the hour I took out the thick slice of bread and the ounce or so of wine that I had brought with to parallel the time of breaking bread together with Pastor Jim, Alicia and all the others present there.

Spiritually, I felt like I was present in Church with Alicia, Pastor Jim and the congregation, not just alone on the mountain in Norway.

My personal time of breaking bread with the Lord lasted way more than just 10 minutes. I thought about the first *'Last Supper'*, how long did it actually last, what all may possibly have been said in addition to what we read about, and what silent thoughts may have went through the disciples minds.

I had eaten the bread a small pinch at a time, together with a small taste of the wine to moisten it. Now mingled together, it reminded me of both his physical suffering and emotional spiritual suffering on that crucifixion day, as Jesus *'paid the death penalty of my sin in full with his own life, ...on my behalf.'*

I had spent well over a half an hour in communion with my Lord and Savior in thankfulness to him. I had eaten all of the piece of bread, and I still had a small portion of the wine left. I had spent my time with my Lord in remembrance of him.

And he laid it upon my heart, to pour out the wine that remained upon the ground. I did this immediately knowing that the wine could not be recovered and put back into the glass again.

The King And The Condemned Prisoner

Then I remembered a story that I was told about a King that attended the execution of a prisoner he had sentenced to death to be sure that he was killed, because he was such a wicked man.

The condemned man asked for a glass of water, which he was given. Holding the glass of water, he was trembling so badly he couldn't even drink it.

In a measure of compassion, the King told him, "Don't worry, take your time, you will not be killed until after you have drunk that glass of water."

The condemned man paused only briefly and then threw the glass of water out upon the ground.

The King realized in a moment, what had just happened. The condemned prisoner had taken the King at his word that he would not be killed until 'AFTER He Drank *THAT* Glass Of Water.'

It was impossible for anyone to gather up the water that had been spilt upon the ground.

The King had to set the man free, because he had given his word that the sentence would not be carried out until '*after he drank **that** glass of water*,' which was now *impossible* because the water that had been poured out upon the ground could not be gathered up and put into the glass again.

In war, blood has been shed and spilt upon the ground for securing freedom for people in many different lands and some has been shed for naught when freedoms are lost or rejected.

It was 34 years ago that I realized his blood was shed for me to secure my eternal freedom. For me and many others who have discovered God's love and forgiveness there is 'Peace In The Valley,' to be rescued and safe on our path forever.

Like the King that '*made himself accountable to a condemned prisoner*' by giving his word that he would not be killed until after he drank '*That glass of water*,' Our God and Creator has made '*Himself Accountable To Us His Creation!*'... by '*Giving us his word*' **in** *his word* that that he has forgiven us forever, giving us *Eternal* Life in the very *moment* we accept (or understand) that Jesus, *paid our debt in full on our behalf.*

The Church In The Midst Of The Nature

7:44 pm My thoughts on 'Church' environment….. Last Sunday in Herredsdalen, I have never seen so Beautiful a Church Building as was displayed in the Mountains with the Lake, the Pasture and a Lamb among the other sheep. The nature fills a portion of the spirit and void in man as we experience his presence in the midst of his creation, for us Norwegians and all others as well when we personally experience it.

We can sense the Majesty of Creation in the Nature. God's message is spoken in and throughout the Nature, and the star filled sky, even if some of us don't fully understand everything about how all of nature exists.

As a Christian I believe I sense the majesty in the nature the same as everyone else does with perhaps an even greater,… or deeper appreciation of him who created it than some people do because I see him as the force in and behind the creation of the nature.

For the people in America who go to church, Christians experience the fullness of his greatness with the presence of the Lord in fellowship/ worship of him, his sacrifice and the humility of the knowledge of our sins forgiven once and for all.

We are reminded of this each week remembering him in the breaking of bread.

Today was special for me to break bread at the same moments Alicia, Pastor Jim and my Brothers and Sisters in Christ were breaking bread in their little Sunday morning gathering.

Some 'Just Religious' people who may never have truly seen Jesus as their own personal savior, might need to feel fulfillment in the physical and spiritual by putting themselves in an environment of 'spirituality' by building Big And Beautiful Churches.

This creates the 'Environment of the Majesty and Awe,' so they can experience a spiritual good feeling coming out of church that satisfies their conscience,... for the moment.

7:59 PM I am sitting here on the mountaintop looking toward Frie. The reflection of the sun has fully brightened one fjord so much that I almost cannot look at it. I wish I had a camera each time I see the beauty displayed in nature by God, and then it changes. The permanent beauty is always present while the clouds, rainbows and the sun on the water and mountain tops change and are always changing....

Just had an odd thought..... the sun's reflection off the water in the fjord is more difficult to look at than directly into the sun...........is it possible that He shines more brightly as he is reflected off from us in our actions of kindness towards others???......Hmmmm.....

Thank You Lord for all the moments of spiritual intimacy with you, and the deeper understanding you reveal to me on every occasion we are present together like this, Amen.

Peaceful Early Morning Thoughts

12th Of July 6:40 AM I have had two coffees and I am writing some more in my book sitting out on the cabin balcony in the perfect stillness after the storm and wind of the night, the sun is bright, the fjord is soft and grayish in color and still, so still,.....

The mountains stand silent and the clouds are soft and nothing is moving, as if they have been painted there. A majestic fog is hanging in the far valley and the sea is absolutely still, a perfect mirror effect. The quiet is almost spiritual in itself.

This is what I believe my Norwegians friends experience in the nature.

I believe all men must experience this in the absence of a personal relationship with God. perhaps it is the closest they can get between the physical/spiritual realm ………. perhaps 'closer' to God in a sense than some who call themselves Christians, but are just 'Religious'.

The 'Only Religious,' and not yet true Christians probably don't even touch on either and only experience the physical response of music and the beauty of an elaborate church building.

My 'One With Nature' Mountain Experience

In all my years of coming to Norway, I have had the privilege of countless Fjelturs. Many of those trips were with a couple friends or a small group of friends, or sometimes just one friend, and many trips were all alone by myself, just listening to the silence of the mountains.

I can hear the voice of God in my thoughts and my heart silently speaking to me in and through the nature as I walk up, or when I sit alone in a quiet place when I get to the top of the mountain. Even just sitting by the seashore, listening to the constant splashing of the waves against the rocks just taking everything in, the nature speaks to my heart.

Many of those 'Special Moments' mountain trips are an experience that is best described by personally experiencing the quietness of the Nature yourself, sometimes with a friend, and sometimes just alone.

My first genuine personal mountain experience began about 8 o'clock in the morning on Sunday, January 23rd, 2005 the day of Martha's mother Dagfrid's 80th Birthday celebration. The Party was to start at 1:00 pm, so I had time to go for a cross country ski tour.

My friend Haldis had suggested that I take a ski tur around Storvatnet, so I decided to take her advice. Storvatnet is a large fresh water mountain lake area just a few kilometers from home. Ola had told me that there was a roadway through the forest to the left side of the lake area that went all the way back to Kanestrøm and also said that I would really enjoy the tour there.

Fortunately there was only a little more than a foot of fresh snow on the skogsvei, making breaking a trail a bit easier. I had a good workout by the time I reached the end of the good part of the trail. I could now see the different homes of Haldis, Torgeir and some other good friends that lived in Kanestrøm across the fjord so I knew how far I had traveled on the skogsvei.

I now checked the time on my mobile phone and was surprised how late in the morning it now was! I quickly realized that I needed to return back to the car as fast as I could so that I would be on time for Dagfrid's birthday party.

It was much easier going back skiing in the tracks that I had made on the way in. I fell into a steady rhythm skiing, pacing myself to what I thought was as fast as I could maintain.

I fell into a dream world of multiple thoughts on the way back, enjoying the new experience of skiing alone in the quietness of the Nature, talking to God silently in my thoughts, grateful for this new and wonderful experience.

It took me the better part of an hour to get back to the car. By the time I returned back to the car, I was free of all worries and more relaxed than I could have imagined possible, even though I had been working very hard skiing as fast as I could through the fresh loose snow. I was so relaxed and peaceful as I put the skis back into the car that I thought, *I need to do this again*!

Then I looked where I was parked and the road leading away from the parking area. This was the first time I had come here so nothing was familiar to look at, especially looking at it from the opposite direction that I had arrived. ......

I was still experiencing my *One with the Nature Experience*..... so much so that I was still in a dream world. ...... I had put the rest of the world completely out of my mind. ..... I wasn't even sure where I was at, or even who I was staying with......I couldn't think of the name of a single friend here for a few moments. ..... I started out with recollecting my thoughts, knowing my name of course and that I was visiting Norway,... then remembering that I was staying with Ola and Martha and everything fell back into place in a few moments. .... And I was still enjoying the peacefulness of what I had just experienced.

My Boat Tour With Ivar Auden

I thought back to February of 1997 on my first trip to Norway when Ivar Auden invited me with him to collect the fish from his dozen or so fish traps he had at different places around Aspøya on the fjord.

An hour into our båttur (baught toor/boat tour), out of curiosity I asked Ivar Auden how long did it take him each time. He said about another hour. Since we had a ways to go to the next trap, I just sat back and settled into the ride.

Somewhere during that time I remembered thinking, this is why people go fishing. It was a peaceful *'Time stands still moment'* even though the boat was scooting along at full speed.

I remembered it now, that during the fishing tour that day, for a few minutes I had touched on a taste of the *One with Nature Experience* that I had feasted on with my ski tour.........Those who have the privilege to go to the mountains often are privileged indeed.

Several Varied Thoughts This Morning

I have written another letter to Pastor Jim, ... I wonder if I will send It?...................

I love Marc as dearly as my son Christopher, and it is Marc that brings Alicia and I together in my heart as a family.

7:00 AM 12th Of July. I have been just sitting here reading a chapter of acts. (the majority decision was not the best.) In some things we must listen to one person, ... or just to the Lord in spite of all others.

Another day, ...another thought or experience, ... what shall the day bring forth???...... I must go down the mountain and tend to the responsibilities of the day, and later I shall be here again.

7:55 AM The sun is starting to warm my face and an occasional small breeze moves the air and reminds me of the cool morning temperature. The sun feels good again when the breeze stops.

This morning could be said to be absolutely perfect in every respect by any person on the face of the earth present in this moment to experience it.

For me, it only lacks 'Perfect Perfection,'....... in that Alicia would be sitting here with me.

100 different friends could be pleasant to have present here and only Alicia sitting here alone with me in this stillness would make this experience the next best thing to heaven on earth for me.

Just to have her here and to be able to look into her eyes, speaking nothing with the mouth, and speaking volumes in a moment of time with just one look into the window of the heart through our eyes. ……..To reach over taking a hold of her hand and to sit here in harmony 'as one in heart, soul and spirit'.…... to me, would be priceless.

'Æ se fram til dagen med.. ikke mer a si.' (I look forward to the day with (Alicia) nothing more to say.)

'Pause'(take a break)…. make a good mocha coffee… and 'pause'… think of nothing for the moment………..

Sometimes I like to deliberately think only in Norwegian, to practice my Norwegian in the thoughts of my mind. My thoughts in Norwegian sometimes seem to be a more affectionate way to express my deepest feelings for Alicia using the simplest of Norwegian words, to say the most.

8:08 AM Only one person, Alicia, can truly fulfill my heart completely, and only Christ can truly satisfy the longings of the spirit and soul. 'pause'……………… and just enjoy taking in all of these wonderful thoughts………………..

8:20 AM On the way down the path from the mountain this morning, I am for a moment feeling a bit lost…….. it seems to be too far to the right, and yet it is a worn path….ahhhh, there is the old dead tree with the white branches on the right, …my safe landmark.

Now I can proceed in absolute confidence. ….. and it is just as important to find those safe "landmarks" in our walk in life, personal and spiritual. It is good to feel reassured and know that you are on the right path.

8:28 AM Waiting for Alicia and I to be restored is to me just waiting for his promises and plan to be fulfilled.….. and I must accept that whatever happens in the future is both his will and plan for each Alicia and me. If, or when, I may have the privilege to have Alicia back in my life, perhaps we could then spend a few days just sitting on the mountain top, just the two of us.

8:32 AM. *Thank You Father, Son, and Holy Spirit for the day 4 January that the Holy Spirit moved Alicia to tell me some of her needs, and for the moment that I made a commitment to you to always fulfill all of her needs that I can. Thank you for the first Sunday we met, our first dinner together. Thank you that my interest in her was so clear that I told her I was not interested in dating her, I was interested in getting married to her. Thank you Lord that Alicia responded immediately, that she felt the same way. Each of us spoke, and the other responded with an instant reply. ….. it is a good plan for life……*

8:47 AM This morning on the way down the mountain, I felt that I was one in spirit with my beloved Alicia.

9:09 AM Communication… or miscommunication?.... Communication can sometimes be so fragile. …….I still wonder what happened between us that we lost each other………??.................??

9:40 AM The mountains and fjords look different from a different point this morning. The same scenery looks different from a farther or closer distance……………perhaps I am too close to my personal situation to see the bigger picture.

Hope

11:50 AM Hope …..To understand hope, is to first understand no hope, not a chance in a zillion, ……for Kristie, Jeremy and Izzy to be together again in this life, … and yet a certain hope for them as Christians of joyful reconciliation in Heaven.

For the ones with no faith or belief in anything there is, in a crisis, nothing but total despair for some people that have lost sight of their hope and they now search for an answer to the pain. Pain and pleasure moves us to do all things, for ourselves or for others. You cannot exist in neutral. We must see the 'something' positive in our lives to hold onto hope. We all need a reason to look forward to the 'something good' in the next chapter of our lives.

I at least have a hope of the possibility of restoration, from someone else's point of view. …… for myself……. I have a certain hope because I believe in Alicia, I believe in myself, in who we are and I believe in us as one according to God's plan. I must only wait and see if I am correct.

11:58 AM Find a higher level of satori in our own company, with our own thoughts. Not just in food or music, it just entertains, or the newspaper, a coffee shop or a pub. Each of these things have their place for each of us in different situations.

It is important to recognize when we are using food for example, to experience that 'Here and Now Moment' of Satori, that feeling of embracing food in the absence of a real hug, or seeking it in alcohol to excess, each of those things holding serious consequences when someone is given to excess. Recognizing these mistakes helps us to make better choices for our life.

Search diligently for that perfect peace of mind and heart, with yourself first, and then with others.

12:24 PM FB Post, A Song: 'Come Running To The Mercy Seat' .... This reminded me of what one young man wrote on his FB page as a tribute to the anniversary of his Grandmothers Passing. "I could always go to Grandma about anything, she always understood and knew what to do."

I can always go to the mercy seat of my Father, He is always there in the same moment that I need him.

Love

9:00 PM Proclaiming the gospel is like proclaiming love for someone, you can be ridiculed, or embraced ....

It is so ironic that the same religious people that would boast of and praise one man's Faithful Love and Devotion to a wife that had left the marriage, ...are the same ones that would condemn a man for his Faithful Love and Devotion (they would now call it an 'obsession') to a girlfriend that broke off the courtship of a relationship............

There Really Is no Difference, Love Is Love, And Devotion Is Devotion.
If you Truly Love someone, ...It is Impossible to stop Loving them.

That is the nature of genuine Love..... To always Love, To always forgive.

To Love is to forgive, and to forgive is to Love.

To Truly Love..... Is to forgive in advance, of any offence that may occur. ....*For*-giveness.........

God's Perfect Love

That is the Nature of God's Perfect Love in that He has forgiven us 'In Advance' of any 'offence', 'wrong doing' or 'sin' that we could ever commit against Him when we 'receive'/'trust'/'accept' that He has 'paid for'/'forgiven' our 'debt' on our behalf.

.... It amazes me that He unconditionally and passionately Loves *every person the same simultaneously* ....When I can only truly relate to Loving one person at a time, more than any other...... Or possibly more than all others put together.

.....Just imagine what it would feel like if God showed you that he loves you 'more than any other person in the world,' ... or that he showed you absolute evidence that he Loved just you, ... More than all the other people in the world put together, *or as if you were* 'The *only person* in the world"........What would you think? ....How would you feel?..... How would you react?..... How would you feel about him now, in the very moment that you realized it. ....

The closest I think we can come to begin understanding a perspective of God's love for every person, is for us to imagine what it would be like for any of us to be able to experience feeling only deep love and compassion for every single person we meet or talk to in our life, ... Or to put it in a human relationship perspective,... That God's love is 'like a man that would fall *passionately, madly in love* with any and every woman he would ever talk to.' ..... whether she was tall, short, slender or not so slender, Beautiful or one that just blended into the crowd....... That *his heart would care about* every woman he would ever meet...... and the *best* example of God's love I can think of from a human perspective, ... is the gentle *Love of a Mother's Heart* for every child she has the privilege to pick up and hold. A mother can *'love them all'* as if they were the *'only child in the world.'*

This is what happened to me the very moment I understood the depth of God's love for me, so many years ago now..... I was speechless in that *'Moment Of My Awakening'*..... My eyes filled with tears, and my heart melted, filled with appreciation that Jesus Loved me so much that he endured my punishment on my behalf.

It was that *moment in time* 34 years ago, that is the reason for my appreciation and Love for Him now forever.

God loves each of us individually 'More than everyone all put together'..... The same as a Mother loves each child 'Totally,' regardless of how many children she has.

A Mother does not 'divide' her love between her children, giving each one less love as more are born to her,.... She *'Multiplies'* her love to each of her children, and loves each and every one 100%, ... seeing each of them being as special as if they were the *'only child in the world.'* A mother *displays* the love of God's heart *in her actions.*

God has multiplied his Love to me and all others he has created, like a Mother multiplies her Love to each child she has *'created.'* ..... His Love for me and all people amazes me.......

Thoughts On Love And Purpose In Life

9:18 PM ....Would she not love me if she knew everything about me, and the thoughts of my heart? and if she did know everything,....... and didn't love... then what?.... where would I go with my hope then?

9:42 PM I just had the thought, it is written, *And he walked with God.* What a privilege it is for me to walk and talk with God all day long, every day as I go about my day's work or activities.

Just like while Alicia is sometimes not on my mind every minute, for sure no hour of the day passes without having many thoughts of her, constantly telling God how I feel and asking him questions about her.

How often do you think of God, or the possibility of God ......or things of eternity??? Things that go on after our mortal lives here are over.

I heard once some study said that the average person thinks about death and the hereafter once every 4 minutes on average, regardless of religion or no religion.

I do not know how to verify that statement or if it is true, but it is true for sure for me,.. I think about spiritual and eternal things constantly, both how it relates to me and how it relates to others both for now and for eternity.

For example, how often does the name of a classmate, old friend or acquaintance come to mind and you think, "Wow.... I have not thought of them for 5, 10 or 20 years!"

.... People that may or may not have had an impact on your life, ...short term or long term. I can think of people that have had a significant influence on my thinking and actions in my life with a single statement of words only, and some that have influenced my thinking... and actions ....by their actions.

I can think of certain special people in my life that have been gone from this life for many years, ...and their words and or actions are still an influence on what I say and do in my daily life now. Actions Speak Louder Than Words.......

It just came to me, my author's name shall be, 'CJ Ford'.....Hmmm, I like that.

10:20 PM, *Father,.. Today, Right Now, I Claim The Power Of Jesus Name To Restore Alicia And I Together Again, If Possible. I Trust You To Establish Forever That Which I Perceived That you Answered Me In Prayer 4 January 2009 From About 10:00 PM Till 10:20 PM.*

10:30 PM. I would never have dreamt that one of the greatest months I have ever experienced in my life would be spent in Norway.

10:34 PM Alone, without the Love of my life and yet in fellowship with the Lord, trusting him for restoration to my Kjærest, beloved Alicia.

Having no earthly hope outside of hope itself and having the most unusual confidence that He and the Holy Spirit already are bringing to pass his glorious plan, of which I may be a small part of with this book, *Love, Life and Hope* and that the understanding given to my heart may be revealed to the hearts of others as well.

Searching For Wisdom And Understanding

..... I just remembered that I asked God for a measure of wisdom some weeks or more ago.

I asked God to give me the 'Wisdom of Solomon.' I reasoned with God that......."Since Solomon didn't need it anymore.......... If He would,........... I would like to have some measure of it bestowed upon me."

.... And I know now that the eyes of my understanding have definitely been opened a little.

To behold the glory and wisdom of God in its entirety would slay a man except one be completely apart from sin, and that can only happen and be experienced fully in Heaven .

10:42 PM There are no tourist's here this week, so as I walked by the schoolhouse I decided to stop and enjoy the moment in the quiet of the day, sitting here on *'our'* balcony at the schoolhouse.

The promise of another day is at hand, as the present day is clearly ending with the gray and silver sunshine reflecting off the edges of the highest clouds.

.... Precious memories of sitting here with Alicia and Marc, ... And Good Night my Love.

10:51 PM…..She is always my hearts bride to me, my greatest and deepest love I have known.

The biggest mountains are small, even with all their Majesty. The still waters of the sea move in and out faithfully responding to God's design for nature.

Each tree is adding only a small bit of beauty to the scenery and any one tree missing will still leave the beautiful forest.

Remove all the individual trees and the forest is lost, so it is with the light of Christians. Just one person's small 'light' (or example) is enough to light another person's way and so it is the actions of each Christian's heart that is important to do their part.

Perhaps just with an encouraging word to another or opening a door for a stranger with a 'Good Morning' to them, and so the more lights there are, the greater chance the 'darkness' of the world vanishes.

Showing Kindness To All

I remember making a decision one day many years ago, that when I laid down to go to sleep each night I wanted to remember that I had shown at least one kindness to at least one stranger that day.

This became a habit and I enjoyed the look on people's faces as they realized that I had purposely waited for a couple of seconds to hold a door open for them even though I wouldn't have had to wait for them.

One day several years ago I saw a person walking down the tinted glass entry hallway at Walmart. I could see the person was carrying two large bags of groceries, so I opened the door at the end of the hallway and waited for them to walk the last 10-15 feet to the door.

I will always remember the surprised look on the woman's face as she turned and walked through the door as I was holding it open for her….. I must have looked just as surprised to her as she came through the door, ….. It was my son's Mother….. we were both too surprised to even say 'Hi.'

While we may bring happiness to a stranger by just saying 'Hi' or 'Good Morning' to them it is equally as important that showing kindness to others, will brighten *your* day, and life as well.

Living Life One Day And One Step At A Time

Tuesday, 13th of July. Another FB post, 'Amazed each day how detailed God is. He orders dates/events when our hand is in his. I see signs and wonders each day. Pray each one finds this relationship with God.'

(My response) 'I was taught to "Take the first step and the next step shall be revealed." The best car headlights cannot shine ahead 100 miles you may need to drive some night, yet they do shine far enough ahead to safely light the path immediately in front of you. Let today's issues and challenges be all you are concerned with to make the decisions today you shall not regret tomorrow.'

13th of July 11:55am In losing Alicia from my present life, God has given me this greater understanding of his desire for restoration of every person he has created, both those who for the first time are seeking for something and those who have experienced that restoration with Him, and later have simply strayed away from communication with Him.

It is my desire through this book to see all men and women drawn to a more appreciative relationship to others, and to each other in each our personal lives and to help each person reading this book to gain a better insight into my personal perspective, and understanding of the Love I have for my God and my Savior...... not just my belief in God.... My Love for Him and all that He has done for me.

A Kiss From A Stranger

I remember back in the fall of 2009 when I was at a small town festival and Tractor Pull one evening a short time after Alicia had taken a step back from the closeness of our friendship.

I was sitting next to a married couple I was acquainted with and I was visiting with them when a friend of theirs walked up to them and started visiting with us while she was waiting for her husband. She asked me who I was and who I was with. I said that I was alone.

I showed her the picture of Alicia, Marc and me that I carried in my pocketbook. I told her that I had lost the love of my life likely in part because I had failed to listen to her and understand what she really was saying in between the words she spoke.

I explained briefly my failure to listen properly, using the example, 'If you borrowed your brothers car, "Drive Carefully" meant "Don't scratch it" and when our parents told us "Drive Carefully" most parents were really saying "I Love You, I want you home safely."'

Only a moment later this woman abruptly placed both of her hands on each side of my face and gave me a kiss right on the mouth! She then said, *"Will you explain that to my Husband!!"* .... I was shocked, both by the kiss from this total stranger to me and by her words........ That I had stumbled onto something that was a bigger problem for many more people than I had realized before now.

Hopefully the understanding I have been given, contained in this book, can draw people together in love, in both the realm of human relationships to each other, and spiritually, to a deeper, and ultimately, a full understanding of God's greater Love for each of us as well.

Commitments Are Commitments

11:58 am The commitment I made to God on 4 January 2009 concerning Alicia stands firm in my heart.

The commitment God made to me and all men is far greater than I can fully comprehend. I have been given enough understanding of it now to realize how much greater it is than the *Full capacity of my understanding*.

I understand fully, and have experienced my commitment to Alicia and it is this human experience of commitment that helps me to more fully appreciate God's much greater commitment of faithful Love He made to me in His Son.

What Image Do You Hold Of God In Your Mind?

12:20 PM 14 July. It is written, *Man is created in the image of God*........ Many men, possibly most men are probably an inaccurate portrayal of God and his Compassionate and Loving nature.

For most of my life before the night of my 23rd birthday, I held this visual image of God in my mind that he looked something like Abraham Lincoln's statue in Washington DC; A stern authoritative image of a Man sitting on a throne handing down judgement to all who got out of line.

I believe that for many of us men, we have often, or at least sometime during our lives acted authoritative, independently stubborn, arrogant and superior, evidenced by one man at a coffee shop or a pub stating that "His wife doesn't know what she is talking about" and his belief that 'he is right' is supported by one or more men in his company stating that "Their wife is the same way."

I personally believe that the reason men are sometimes so 'Macho' is because it is the devil's way of making man appear contrary to the heart and mind of God, and the gentleness of God's compassionate love for us is hidden.

God is merciful, kind and compassionate. .... Thinking about people I know that are merciful, kind and compassionate, ... A lot more women's names come to mind than men's names ....*A LOT more.*

Did God Make Women *Smarter* Than Us Men?

.....After thinking about all of these thoughts and more, ... over and over in my mind,

...... *'Fast Forward into the Future,'* .... To more than 3 months later in October of 2010 back in Wisconsin.

I was talking with Morten one morning as we were driving to another farm to start combining corn. We were having one of our frequent 'mobile truck office' conversations about many different subjects, of which that day we were discussing the differences between men and women and how we think and react differently.

Morten and I not only worked together, he was like my brother to me. I was treated like family at Lisa's home. We had all become the best of friends over the many years since we met, so much so that Lisa would introduce me to her friends as Morten's brother from the other Mother.

I had told Mort about many of the things that I had written about in my book. Talking about how God had made us men and women so different physically, strength wise and emotionally.

All of a sudden I said, "Mort, ... Do you think it is possible that God made women smarter than men???" .... after only a couple moments thought Mort said, "....I don't know, ... I've never given that any thought, ... I'll have to think about that a bit."

I replied back to him, "...Well, ……. If he did, … how would we know??!!!" ………. "I mean, you and I know that we are both intelligent and we are able to have a lot of in depth conversations about a lot of different things. If some normal looking adult walked up to us and as soon as they started to talk to us, we both knew in an instant that they only had the mentality of a simple young child, we would both look at each other and think, 'They're not all there.'"

"But, …..THEY would look at us as equal to themselves and not understand that we were 'smarter' than them." …………… I then said to Mort, "What if that is the way women look at us, …….. What if they just tolerate us and keep us for pets??"… Mort said *"That's* something to think about for a while."

What Is The Difference Between Men And Women?

'Fast Forward again' to August of 2011. I am back in Norway for the summer, sitting at my desk with the copy of my original *Love, Life & Hope* manuscript reading some of it and thinking about the differences between how men and women think and act. Why do we men and women have such a challenge to just get along together and understand each other?? ………..

The thought crossed my mind about the book that was titled *Men are from Mars, Women are from Venus*. I knew from the title that the book was likely meant to suggest that men and women are as different as if we were from two different planets.

As I thought about just the books title (because I haven't read any of the book or even held one in my hand) I said out loud to the Lord, "That can't be Lord, because we are both human beings, from the same planet, ……… We are the same, …...and yet different at the same time."

I also had a new spiral notebook in front of me, wondering how to start an introduction to the book because starting with the first page of my manuscript would be like starting in the middle of the movie without understanding how we got there.

The XX & XY Data

.... I sat there for a long time, reading and thinking about all of the thoughts that I had written the previous summer, ... all of a sudden only one question seemed to be dominant in my mind,........ 'What is the difference between men and women??'

I thought about and searched my mind for an answer to that question, until I suddenly said out loud, ... "Lord,.... *What IS the difference between men and women??"* ......

A moment later He gave me the answer echoing in my thoughts, *"XX chromosome, XY chromosome."* So I wrote a big 'XX' and 'XY' on each half of the top of my first sheet of paper in the book.

.... I just stared at the XX and XY for a while and I said in my thoughts, *"Well Lord, ... It's just 4 letters, and the 'Y' is just an 'X' with one leg missing".*..............

"The two 'XX's' have 8 legs of DNA and the 'XY' has only 7 legs of DNA." ... Logical observation.

..... I thought about that for a few moments longer and no other thoughts came to me so I just divided the 7 into the 8, and the answer was 1.142%, a logical answer to the different amount of DNA between and man and a woman. ....

..... I stared at the 1.142% answer only a moment more and I blurted out loud, *"LORD!,..... A Woman has 14% more DNA than I do!!!,..............* *WHAT'S IN THERE??!!!"* ......?????

.... As I thought about this, I thought about several possibilities..... Is there something special in this 'missing leg' of DNA from men? .....or is it just 'extra' data? ....

My next thoughts were, *'No, of course the entire 'Y' is different data that women don't have'* ....*'The 'Y' is what makes a man a man.'*....'The physically bigger, muscular makeup.'.......

...... Is it the 'Y' data that is the *'unemotional,' 'logical,' 'calculated'* thinking we men do? The *'Gittrrrr Done'* side of our thinking???

Were Women Created By Nature With A 'Sweetheart' Personality?

Is it the *'X' data* that contains the *'emotionally compassionate, logical'* side of our makeup? ....The compassion, gentleness and kindness generally associated with a *woman's nature?*

.... Then I thought, *"If this is so, ... then 'Women have a 'DOUBLE Dose' of tenderness and compassion in the 'X' data, ... And we men have only 'HALF a Dose' of the tenderness and compassion that women have."*

If the differences in our basic emotions and thinking abilities between men and women *are actually wrapped up in the chromosome makeup,* the 'Y' being 'logical,' less emotional, unemotional, ...(or,...'*insensitive?'...*) ... and the 'X' being emotional, gentleness, kindness and compassion, ...
Then *all* women *'would be/are by nature,'* ....*'All Sweethearts!!!'*

.........*and if any man complained* that his wife/woman/girlfriend were the *'opposite'* of a 'Sweetheart'........ It is likely possible, or *probable* that it is *he,* or *some other man* in her life's experience that has pushed her into a corner emotionally, mentally or physically, suppressing or destroying her 'Sweetheart' nature, and has *forced her to react defensively* to protect her heart's feelings. .... (Something for us men to think about *before* we complain about our wife or girlfriend................*Jus' sayin.'*)

If our personality as men is *actually* made up of one half coming from the compassion, gentleness and kindness from our X chromosomes and one half coming from the less emotional or unemotional logical thinking side of our Y chromosomes, then it would seem 'logical' from my point of view that we should be able to *'choose'* to lean to one side or the other of our two 'X&Y' natures, thus that being the emotional (X) or unemotional (Y) natures.

It would seem to me that the answer to the *nature that prevails* or at least is more dominant is revealed from a story I was told about the wisdom of an Indian Chief speaking with his son. He told the boy that there was a war between two animals, 'A Raging Wolf and A Gentle Fawn' within him, striving to control the boy as he grew into a man. The boy asked 'Which one wins?' The Chief answered 'The one you feed.'

Gods Special Gift To Women

I have now wholeheartedly come to believe that God has given women two things that most of us men in general either do not possess, …..or at least we usually do not exhibit.

First, He has given women the ability to 'Multi-task' better than men.

God knows everything about everything simultaneously (like 'Santa Claus' is portrayed).

While God holds 'millions of thoughts' in his mind simultaneously, I have come to understand that he has given all, (or most) women a small portion of this wonderful ability. He has given women the ability to hold and focus on up to a 'half a dozen or more thoughts at one time.'

Second, God has given women a *greater measure of His Nature* or 'Compassion of the Heart' than we men have in general, or… at least that we men allow ourselves to openly express.

A Unique Eye Opening Experience For Me

……. *'Fast Forward again'*… To one day in the future, in May of 2012, when I would gain this insight through a unique experience driving down a long straight stretch of Minnesota highway between Caledonia and Spring Grove that would *forever change my understanding* about the basic difference between the way that men and women think.

The absence of sharp turns, blind corners and traffic allowed me to drift a bit deeper into thought.

For about 20-30 seconds or so, I was thinking about 'Alicia, my book, organic farming, my Grandchildren and stopping for a coffee in Spring Grove!' *simultaneously!!*… As if I were on top of a mountain in Norway looking down and seeing *all five of these thoughts in one perspective!!*

When the 'Multiple Thinking' experience ended abruptly, I said out loud, *"WHOA!! Lord !! … THAT was quite an experience!!!!"*

Five seconds later, still spellbound by the experience, my phone rang and it was a friend from Arkansas that I hadn't talked with for several months.

I answered the phone without saying 'Hi.' I just said, *"NANCY!!, I was just thinking about F-I-V-E things, SIMUTANEOUSLY!!!….. All at ONCE!! …………Is that the way women think?????"* …….

Nancy immediately replied, *"Well DUH….. How do you think we get everything done?!!!"*

Now I *KNEW* that I was onto *'Something'* about understanding at least some of the difference between men and women and how we *think* differently, … and how that probably has *something* to do with how and why we *act and react differently!* ….. Now the question in my mind was *"WHY did God make us so different in so many ways??"*

Two Stories To Help Us Men Understand The Difference In Our Thinking

As a result of this 'Less than half a minute long' eye opening revelation, I 'Made up two little stories' to bounce off some of both my men and women friends to gain some more insight into whether I was on track to understanding something about this unique difference between men and women and how we think,… alike at times, and most of the time differently.

A woman saying that she has *'A half a dozen things on her mind today'* is an *ENTIRELY* different thing than a man saying he has 'A half a dozen things on his mind today'.

The stories I 'made up' to help us men understand this difference are as follows.

For the first *'Story'* example: For most men it is like he is watching '6 television channels at one time.'

His *'thinking'* is like *channel surfing,* bouncing back and forth between 6 channels catching bits and pieces of 6 movies playing at the same hour, or *focusing entirely* on one movie *(or project)* at a time (…*Gittrrrr Done…*) until he has watched all 6 movies.

Basically for most women, It is like she can *'See all 6 channels simultaneously'* and *'Hears' all 6 conversations simultaneously, comprehending all of it…. Simultaneously!…..*

For the second *'Story'* example: Parents have 6 children and the youngest child stubs her toe and starts crying.

If the father is there, he picks her up, holds her tight and consoles her, oblivious to most everything else going on in the house, while he gives her *100% of his attention and affection.*

If the father is not home, the mother in the same situation, picks the young child up and gives her the *'exact same 100% attention and affection'* ...... while at the *same time* is aware of where every other child is at in the house, what they are doing,(yes, Mother has *'eyes in the back of her head'* as the saying goes) if any of them are near the stove where she has water boiling, ... *AND at the SAME TIME is planning a Birthday party for the day after tomorrow!!*

Reactions To My Stories

I started bouncing these 'two stories' off both men and women for their reaction to see if I was on track to understanding this amazing, and intriguing difference between men and women.

I told the 'story' of the father/mother and little girl to one friend Sue, from Oregon, that I was a sales associate with in one company.

When I mentioned *'Planning a birthday party at the same time'*... Sue burst out laughing loudly over the phone and she then said, (still laughing) *"Oh my God!!... What am I going to do with you now that you've got us figured out!!!"*

..... Knowing that I was truly *'ON to Something'*... I told both stories to several other men and women friends, to confirm my conclusions. I preferred to tell the stories in person to both men and women so I could watch their reactions on their faces and in their eyes.

The moment that a woman got that *'Oh My!' look on her face and in her eyes,* I *knew* she had just realized that I had at least a basic understanding of this unique difference between a man and woman's ability to think on a singular or multiple level. *I KNEW,* that *she KNEW,* that I now *understood something* about what she had *known all the time.*

When I told the same stories to men, a few men looked at me with a blank stare like... *"What* are you talking about??" Some of the men responded in general *"...That's an interesting perspective..........."*

A Reason And Answer To My Question

.... It was a call to my friend LaCinda that confirmed the *reason for this unique difference* between men and women's thinking abilities for me.

As I said the 'boiling water/nearest kid in danger' part of the second story, LaCinda cut me off in the middle of my story saying, "Curt! Curt! You don't have to explain it to me, ……..all you have to say is 'Motherhood'.…..." ……… *MOTHERHOOD!!!!!!!!* ……. *Of COURSE God made women different!* ….. *MOTHERHOOD!!!!…..* *Survival of the young!!!!……..*

In a moment more I realized that God *most likely* had given this same wonderful ability of multiple thinking awareness to every, or most every female in every species,….. *Motherhood!!….. Survival of the Fawn!!….* The Doe deer has to be aware of *everything in her environment around her simultaneously, for the survival of the fawn!!…..* And the Buck *probably* is really only just interested in having sex once a year,……... *Jus' Sayin'*…..

I have come to the point now *'In The Future'* that every time I tell a woman these two stories, I feel like *I am the student 'Teaching' the Teacher, what she has known all along.*

Hearing The Words, *And… Understanding The Message*

Listening, ……. We men do not *listen*…….. Thinking again about driving to church that one Sunday morning in May of 2009 when Alicia asked me, *"What did I just say two sentences ago."* Normally the one asking that question planned to say *"Gotcha."*…. But I repeated the sentence back to her almost word for word. Alicia said "Good, I just wanted to see if you were listening."

………. I repeated her words back to her, but I realize now that I was not actually listening to the message of what she was *really saying* between the words, which was the most important. …….. Like when she told Marc and I standing on the cliff of the river's edge in Norway, ……………. *"Don't go so Close!"* ………….. I wish I could go back and re-live that day so I could walk over to her, give her a big hug and a kiss and say, *'Marc and I Love you too!'.*

12:52 PM Sometimes I feel that my life has been like an athlete in training. It takes months and years of disciplined training just to be prepared for one week in the Olympics.

As I recall the things that I have experienced the past 30 to 40 years, I understand now that because of the challenges I have experienced throughout my life, I can now draw from those memories to understand and make sense of the events that have transpired the most recently.

It is the connection of our life experiences for each of us that helps us to appreciate the good things in our present lives and helps us get through any challenging events to get to the next good thing in life that awaits us.

Drawing from the experience in our memories of the past, and what we may be experiencing in our present situations we have the opportunity to choose to enrich our present lives, blending the two together. I understand now how this has prepared me to receive into my heart the understanding I am now being given.

Love Is Faithful

1:01 p.m. I know now that even if Alicia were never to be back together with me, I will always love her. It is because of the unconditional Love I have experienced for Alicia that I am able to understand more fully how that God loves each and every person in the world, even if they have rejected him and His Love in the past,.... And it is his desire that we all can now understand His Love for us.

The story of my love for Alicia is easily understood by all men and women because we all have experienced these emotions at some level of intensity.

It is similar to the much greater story of God's proclamation of love for every person, and that he gave everything for us.

Even as this book helps you to understand the depth of my love for Alicia, and my devotion and commitment to her, it will also help you understand the depth of my love for my Savior in that he first loved me, and gave everything for me, and He Loves You the same. The words of the book speaking, become like a small story of the much greater love in the gospel message.

1:04 p.m. Faithfulness begins in the heart. Faithfulness is the foundation of love. In love, it is *our actions* that reveal the secrets and faithfulness of our heart.

In salvation, it is *the action* the Lord took on our behalf, even before we understood it, that reveals the *Love and Compassion in the heart and mind of God for us*, and salvation is a result of the understanding of God's faithfulness of love provided to us in Jesus. It was that moment in time 34 years ago, that changed my life and destiny forever.

Joyfulness In The Heart Overrides Physical Pain

1:25 p.m. I am done checking fences, and my legs are soaking wet and cold up past my knees. It is kind of funny that I was not even aware of it until this moment…. It is the outcome of being happy in Him.

When I started walking along the fence in the wet grass, the bottoms of my pants around my ankles' became wet and uncomfortable, but I started to think that uncomfortable was not unbearable and I thought about both the joyfulness I had experienced from Alicia's love and the joyfulness I experience when I think about my Saviors Love for me.

As much as I know that I love Alicia, I know that my Savior loves me more, even more than I am able to fully comprehend. The joyfulness of these two thoughts dissolved any misery or unpleasantness I could have, either physical or emotional. …….

Boiling Water Explosion

In the early Nineties I experienced the terribly painful boiling water injury to my left arm that I briefly mentioned previously.

I did 'Custom Silage Harvesting' for other farmers and I had a Self-Propelled Forage Harvester that had the motor and the cooling radiator mounted on the back of the machine covered by a big flat hood over the top with the radiator cap sticking out of a hole in the hood.

Every morning I would service the machine and check all the fluid levels including the radiator water level.

We had worked late into the night to finish filling the corn silage bag because it was going to snow overnight and we were just finishing as it started snowing hard in the early morning hours.

As I started to service the machine when I returned later in the morning after daylight, the farmer came over and said that he needed a little more silage to finish filling the bag, about enough to fill a heaping pile in the back of a pickup box.

This would only take me a few minutes to do so I just went and chopped a small pile on the wagon, unhooked and went back to servicing the machine.

When I went to check the water level in the radiator I climbed up on top of the machine and walked back to the end of the hood, bent over and reached down to unscrew the radiator cap. Normally running the motor for less than 5 minutes would barely bring the motor up to near a normal engine temperature.

.... Unknown to me, the last few minutes of harvesting in the snowfall the night before had plugged the radiator completely with a mixture of corn leaves and snow.

In the few minutes I used the harvester that morning it brought the motor temperature up to boiling hot, just to the brink of overflowing, which would have warned me that the water was scalding hot.

..... The moment I just loosened the radiator cap a little, it exploded into my hand sending a stream of boiling hot scalding water up my wrist underneath my long sleeved shirt nearly up to my shoulder, simultaneously spraying all over my face and neck.

In less than 2-3 seconds I quickly unbuttoned my shirt sleeve and pulled it up to get the hot soaking wet sleeve off my arm. *Two seconds later I watched all the skin on my left arm slide down my arm into my hand.*

My very first thought as I looked at that handful of my own skin laying in a crumpled mess in my hand was, *NOW I understand* why Mothers and Grandmothers are so paranoid about keeping small children with their tender, tender skin away from boiling water on the stove.

The level of pain was something I had never imagined before now. I immediately dropped the handful of still very hot scalded skin and made a tight fist attempting to alleviate some of the pain.

I had lost so much skin from my wrist and up my arm that as I tightened my arm muscles, large drops of blood appeared on my wrist and some smaller drops farther up on my arm.

I immediately thought of the verse that says *'He sweat as it were great drops of blood.'* .... *I simply cannot imagine the stress or agony* that would cause a man to sweat blood through our normal several layers of skin...............

My face and neck skin fared better, only turning as bright red as a very bad sunburn, spared from the same scalding, likely because the thin 'spray of water' had a fraction of a second to lose a few degrees of temperature to the air as it passed through it.

I went to the house on the farm where the farmers' wife tried putting on some different remedies for the pain to no avail.

Temporary Pain Relief

I then jumped into my truck and drove home where I had a skin care product that I sold through an MLM company that I remembered they said was also good for serious burns....... I was anxious to find out to say the least!!

When I got home and applied the skin care cream, instantly nearly 100% of the pain was gone!!

I was actually excited in those few moments that I had burned my arm! Because now I had my own 'Personal Testimony' that the product really worked and I would be able to more successfully market it, so I was seeing $$ signs of blessing from my accident.

...... But in about 5 minutes the burning pain returned, so I applied more product and again the pain disappeared, for about 5 minutes.

I repeated this about a half a dozen times with the same recurring results. I now realized that I needed to go to the Doctor.

A Deeper Understanding Of Suffering

As I drove out of the driveway the burning pain returned, to a new level of intensity. It was so overwhelming that it caused me to think about the unimaginable excruciating level of pain my Lord Jesus must have endured on the cross as he bore the penalty of my sins and offences against God.

I was humbled before my Savior as I thought about that he *voluntarily chose to take the punishment that I deserved*...........that I *knew* was a far, far more incomprehensible level of pain than anything I was experiencing at the moment. ....

I thought about him in so much agony, with nails driven through the joints of his wrists' and ankles by the soldiers, *to deliberately inflict the maximum amount of pain and suffering possible.*

A Deeper Understanding and Appreciation Gives Birth To Greater Joyfulness

As I thought about all of this while I was driving to the doctor, tears ran down my face and I started to sing out loud, songs of Praise, Thankfulness, Gratefulness and Love for my Savior........

As I did this my joyfulness and appreciation of his Love for me overrode, or 'softened' my pain to the level that I actually *'enjoyed' experiencing the painful arm* because it gave me such insight into the suffering that Jesus endured for me.

My greater joy in thinking of him overcame my physical situation. I now understand that greater joy, that just like the apostle Paul, regardless of the circumstances he found himself in, nothing mattered to him in the physical realm, his joyfulness of the heart overcame all physical feelings.........

Broken Hearts Are More Painful Than Physical Suffering

7:16 AM 14th of July Facebook post by a young woman. "Morning sickness, again"....... These three words say so much, and say it all........ The morning sickness will come to pass,... A Child is on the way, and a Mother is in waiting.

Just thinking of things that never leave our thoughts. Thinking again of our neighbors who just lost their 49-year-old son in a small plane crash, giving a ride to a young groom to be married Saturday. Flying low, a downdraft dropped the plane out of the sky. Both men were lost.

What started out as a joyful time of celebration for many, in a moment of time turned into a time of mourning, for everyone involved.

I am sick to my stomach with sadness for John and Joran losing their son, and all the friends and family of the young Bride and Groom, and the young Bride-to-Be whose anticipated future was no more.

How many people, ourselves included, have at some point in our lives' suffered sorrow so deep that we are sick to our stomachs....... As I think about this again now, I get sick to my stomach the same as when I first heard about it.

Turn Negatives Into Positives

Facebook post on 'Dyslexia' I wrote: 'I am acquainted with a man who says that someone at his school diagnosed him with dyslexia or attention deficit disorder or something like that as a young 6-year-old child because he was daydreaming and not paying attention in class.

He said that he felt bad because they told him he had to stay in from recess for a special class and he wanted to go out and play with the other kids. He says his mother decided to refuse to accept that label about him and told the school so.

He now teaches, in addition to other principles and perspectives, that it is important *to believe in our own abilities*, in part because *his mother believed in him, and taught him* to never accept limitations or 'Labels' placed upon us by others.'

It is not necessarily bad to feel a particular emotion, 'bad' or 'good'. It is important to recognize what the feeling is and how it affects you.

It is good to have experienced the freezing cold in order to fully appreciate the warmth of a blazing hot fire in the stove or a fireplace.

I have likewise come to appreciate more, the joyfulness and blessings in my life, because of walking the path of loneliness.

As I have went from one to the other and back again, I have learned to accept and embrace the 'aloneness,' knowing that it will pass and I will remember the days of my lonesomeness and appreciate even more the days of blessings and happiness.

The Power Of A Woman's Prayer

15th of July 10:20 AM The thought just came to me again as if it were spoken as a proclamation echoing in a large auditorium …. *"Never Underestimate The Power Of A Woman's Prayer."*

The Lord seems to be emphasizing this statement much more than the last time this thought came to me. Maybe I wasn't listening the first time to the importance of the message contained within these words…. the power of a mother praying with the love and compassion in her heart.

……. I have heard some men pray with a tone of *'Authority'* as if God was supposed to listen to them because of their eloquent words and the length of their prayers. ….. I have heard some women clergy do the same.

……. *'Effective prayer'* is when we humbly pray with our hearts to ask God for 'favors' or 'Blessings',…….. Sometimes for someone else, who maybe does not even know that we are praying for them, …and we expect nothing for ourselves.

…..I believe that too often we men have prayed for things selfishly, in part because of our human nature.

I believe that God has given women a greater understanding and a deeper experience in prayer than most men because of the measure of the nature of His heart that he has given them in 'Motherhood' displayed in the compassion of caring for children and the elderly, both her own, and others, this gentleness and compassion of her heart spilling over into her prayers.

I have heard this difference in listening to both men, and women praying, listening to the tonality and tenderness of her words when a woman prays with her heart.

10:28 AM I also believe that God has given women a unique higher level of compassion and understanding that most of us men can *ever fully enter into.* I feel fortunate to have caught a significant glimpse of it.

King Solomon

It is proclaimed about King Solomon, that he was the wisest man in the world. He is known for his decision as the Judge of the land for determining the truth and settling a dispute between two women.

Two Mothers were sleeping in the same tent, each with their infant child at their side.

The one mother apparently accidentally laid upon and smothered her child. Seeing this upon waking, she laid her dead child next to the other woman and laid the live child next to herself.

Upon waking, the real Mother of the live child was at first distraught at the dead child next to her, and then recognized that the dead child was not hers.

In the dispute over the live child, the argument came before King Solomon.

Listening to the two women both claiming to be the mother of the live child, he commanded a sword be brought and he would divide the live child in two so each mother could share the child equally.

The real Mother immediately surrendered the child to the other woman to save the child's life.

King Solomon said "Give the child to her, she is the mother."

The King knew that the real Mothers love for her child's safety would identify her.

Solomon *'thought'* compassionately like a *Mother*,

...like a woman.

He used the 'Wisdom of a Woman'

And the 'Heart of a Mother'

To determine the truth.

King Solomon's *'Wisdom,'*

... Was that he 'thought' like a Mother would think,

.... 'He thought like a Woman would think.'

.... Something for us Men to think about.

I have come to the place where concerning deeper thinking and insight, ...that God has indeed given Women a greater measure of wisdom and insight than most of us Men on many, ...or most issues.

When we as Men and Women, *embrace each other's strengths, we can become a greater force for good together than either of us can be as individuals.*

Uncertainties And Reassurance

10:30 AM My thoughts.... Recurring fears of sadness, what if Alicia and I will not get back together?

... If I think about my prayer on the 4th of January in my total surrender and commitment to the Lord that night that his plan, his perfect plan and will be done, ... I have to trust that he will one day either restore our relationship, or give each Alicia and I blessings in our separate lives.

At least He has given me peace again with these thoughts............

11:10 AM All men are born, and eventually die. ...... It is only important what good you can do in between those two events.

Questions And Answers

11:15 AM Ola and I were having breakfast this morning having a conversation about some very in depth subjects and Ola said "You ask more questions than a Wise Man can answer" ....hmmmmm......... *'Ask a question that a wise man cannot answer??'*..... Something to think about, and that was quite insightful of him to make that comment.

..... I often know "The answer", or "An answer" to the questions I ask.

......Asking a question sometimes provokes the other person to think about a logical answer for themselves and possibly how the answer to the question may pertain to them.

Sometimes the answers to questions have more value to us if we come up with conclusions ourselves rather than someone telling us an answer.

Thought Provoking Questions

11:16 AM The *'Wisdom'* sometimes *'Is in the Question!'* not in the answer. Can you ask yourself a question that you cannot answer? How would that change your life, *with,* or *without* the answer to your question?

Fast Forward into the Future again: One day I would meet a college electronics teacher early one cold March morning at a small town café, as I traveled through Gurley Nebraska, on my way to a two day seminar in Denver. We had an interesting visit and we asked each other many thought provoking questions regarding the various subjects we touched on in our brief 2 hour visit.

He said that he quickly knew who would be the top students in his class by the quality and depth of thought they put into their questions.

Much of life is about questions and answers. Sometimes we make jokes about it.......Perhaps, because we do not have the answers to those questions....and we don't know what else to say.

Pleasures In Life

11:19 AM We are traveling along the road this morning after crossing Halsafjord on the ferry.

Every trip over a fjord on the ferry is a wonderful experience to me, even on some of the ferry routes that I have traveled countless times. I have traveled some of these roads so many times that I have become familiar with nearly every turn in the road in some places here.

I have traveled much and have had a full experience in Norway, and even that is only a taste of life. Many of us only taste what others live, both good and not as good.

A rich man's life is presumably filled with happiness, or so perceived so by many of those who are not as rich as some are.

For example, I believe some people smoke and drink because they see rich people doing that, and in truth regarding smoking for example, a poor man can enjoy a cigarette just as much as a rich man. And so for those few moments the poor man is living a rich man's life, he has achieved the satori he seeks, even if only for a few moments at a time.

And yet death and sorrow, knows no man rich or poor, and both men also experience each of those things the same.

L-i-s-t-e-n / S-i-l-e-n-t

11:34 AM Listening to some people you can learn. If people are intolerant to listen, People are also likely intolerant to learn. Sadly I used to be one of them.

.... It is interesting that the same letters that spell the word 'Listen' .... Also are the *SAME* letters that spell the word 'Silent'! .... Something to Think About.

Sharing Life's Experiences

11:40 AM We are driving past a friend Ole's house. As Ola pointed out Ole's white house he said that the yellow house near there serves a fish dinner. He said it is also a kind of a fish museum and somewhat of a special experience to eat there.

I would like to stop there one day and experience that, but more importantly I would like to share that with Alicia......

Do you want to just enjoy life's experiences yourself, or is it important that you share those experiences with someone, or a special someone?.......

Actually each of those scenarios can be a great experience, for different people,.... I believe that for most of us, Happiness shared, is Happiness multiplied. ....

In the first scenario, each of us can usually enjoy most things for whatever enjoyment is in it for ourselves.

Secondly, most of us enjoy having a traveling companion or good friend with on a trip, each of us enjoying the sightseeing trip at a different level for each our own interests, and a shared enjoyment.

Third, and best I think, is when we not only enjoy the sights and sounds of an experience ourselves, but we experience great contentment in bringing happiness and pleasure to the one special person in our life, that also including our children if we have a family.

A good family experience is when we experience something together, 'As one, in spirit.' ....I am thinking back to the special moments of joyful laughter I shared with Alicia and Marc at the cabin.

..... I still remember the feeling of great happiness and contentment in my heart enjoying seeing each of them in their individual happiness of laughter and at the same time enjoying the moment between all three of us as one, in a happy joyful spirit, a precious memory for me.....

Mountain Waterfalls

12:16 PM Driving past the mountain streams coming down from the top of the mountains gives me hope, ... somehow, the very sight of the beautiful waterfalls gives me hope in everything. The water just keeps coming down and the stream appears to come from nowhere and yet there has to be something that feeds the water into the stream from above. .... sometimes things are not what they appear to be at first. ......

When I first saw a waterfall coming down from the very 'Top' of the mountain my only conclusion was that it must be a huge spring of water coming up from within the earth.

...... But, after seeing so many waterfalls on nearly every mountain, it seemed impossible that there could be that many springs yielding up so much water. It seemed that what I was seeing was only 'Half of the Story'.

I just enjoyed the beauty of it without questioning the source of the water.

The simple explanation and answer came when I finally out of curiosity one day asked Ola as we were passing an enormous waterfall beginning right at the 'Top' of the mountain, "How can so much water come down from the top of the mountain?"

He said "That is not the top of the mountain. Many of the 'Mountain Tops' that you see from the valley, are only the 'Shoulder' of the mountain. The 'Top' of the mountain is many kilometers back and the snowmelt water can flow for 50 kilometers or more."

I thought about the water trickling slowly along before plunging down over the 'shoulder' of the edge of the mountain with a deadly force, sometimes harnessed by the water turbine and converted into useful electric power. With the waters power now spent, it flows harmless and quietly to the ocean waiting for the wind and sun to restore its power .

…….. Once we now learn the truth about anything, we cannot go back to a state of innocence, ignorance or disbelief about that subject, be it physical, emotional or spiritual.

Priorities / Reflections

12:20 PM There's a song on the radio. I wasn't really listening closely, but I heard some of the words to the song…... It was something like My Heart has no time for memories of you….

There's always time for what is most important, if that person was really ever important in our life ….. We all make time for whatever is important, or whoever is important to us, or most important to each of us. Our actions confirm or deny whatever we may say with our words.

12:38 PM …… *'Lead me beside the still waters,'* just came to the thoughts in my mind as we are passing by a long narrow swamp with crystal clear water in it like a fresh water creek.

It is absolutely still without a ripple and the cattails stand quietly in the middle……… It is good to be reminded of this quiet place of refuge. … Sometimes our hearts and our minds just need a few moments of peaceful quiet and rest.

12:54 PM ……………… I wonder, if I will always wait for Alicia to be back with me, or if I will find another relationship that is enough to be content, peaceful, and happy?……….

I'm still not sure why we are apart, if I hurt her feelings or she is afraid of something, or if I am not good enough.

…… If we could just sit down and talk over a pot of coffee, so I could understand how she feels. I feel certain things would work themselves out and the uncertainties would just melt away.

.... If it is that I am not good enough now, why would I be good enough later ....?

The Greater Purpose Of This Book

1:19 p.m. *Love, Life and Hope*, ... What is important to write in the forward to this book? Do I index the book into separate sections of *'Love and Life' / 'Life and Hope'/ 'Love and Hope?'* Different sections that gives something to all people?

Do I organize the book into different chapters, etc. To fit together with what I have been experiencing?

....Or do I just leave it written as one long story of my experiences??

...... The most important thing seems to be that anyone and everyone who reads this book will now have a deeper understanding of their own life.

A Peaceful Quiet Experience By The Sea

1:43 PM Valset. We have to wait one half hour for the next ferry so I have decided to take a walk. There is a large solid rock mound that is fenced off from the parking area and my curiosity has compelled me to see what is out there.

I walked around the fence and found what looked like a hiking trail back upon the massive Rock peninsula that extended out into the sea. The rocks were high enough that if you were walking along the water on one side you could not see over them to the ship on the other side. I walked along the top observing everything I could.

I walked completely out to the end and sat down upon the rocks in a position that I could watch the ferry boat coming across the fjord and calculated the time that I would need to get back to the truck to board the ferry in a timely fashion.

In the meantime I enjoyed the absolute still and quiet peacefulness where the only noise was the gentle wind creating small ripples of water splashing upon the rocks.

The large smooth rocks that are well above the sea level seem to tell a different story of this quiet, tranquil place. The wind and water worn rocks bear evidence of violent winter storms that have beaten the edges of the rocks smooth over countless years.

Right now I feel a little like those large smooth rocks. ….. Just sitting here in the sunshine with nothing having much effect on me positive or negative, just existing in a peaceful, neutral state of mind…… having been through the storms of life, enjoying now the present warm and calm weather.

…. And knowing that the cold winter and storms will return in their seasonal cycles, I can take advice from a common Norwegian saying, *"Det er ikke dårlig vær, bare dårlig klær."* (There is no bad weather, just bad clothes.) Dress properly for the cold and take shelter from the storm and we will survive just fine.

……. We can take the same advice for our personal life and emotional needs. Show Love and compassion, and be willing to receive Love and compassion…….

Knowing that we are Loved and cared about by someone in our life helps us to survive the storms of life we sometimes experience.

Knowing that God loves us and cares about us helps us to survive the emotional storms of life….. even if we face those storms alone.

I cannot see any of the cars from where I am sitting and so I am alone for a few moments watching the sun dance upon the water in the quietness of the nature with just the gentle splashing of the waves to listen to.

I only occasionally glanced at the ferry boat coming across the fjord towards me. It is just gliding as graceful as a sailboat would coming across the water, and gradually the faint, and yet growing hum of the boat motor gives evidence of its approach.

I do not want or need to look at the time, for it seems that at this moment, time is standing still,……. I want this moment to last longer.

As I close my eyes, the feeling that I am experiencing takes me back to the quiet times I shared with Alicia. The good memories of the stillness we experienced sitting in the back yard with a cup of coffee in our hands looking up at the majesty of the universe displayed in the star filled night sky, sharing our thoughts….. Alicia, if you were only here to share this with me……..

The fjord is so wide that I cannot see anything immediately on the other side, just the distant low mountains. The beauty of the fjord in this present place fills my heart with a measure of contentment.

I am enjoying the present moment, the beauty that is before my eyes and at the end of my fingertips, so near to me it seems that I could reach out and touch it.

The width of the fjord is like the length of our lives, so far off that we cannot see what it holds for us. We cannot yearn for what is so far off that we cannot have it yet.

We must enjoy the present moment while we have it, and before we lose it forever.

The only thing of beauty missing here for me right now would be to look into Alicia's eyes. For me...... Right now....... it is everything.

Perfect Contentment In Everything

1:55 PM The ferry boat is getting nearer and demands my return to the truck.

As I casually walk back across the large flat rocks on top of this little Peninsula, I am extremely contented, it was well worth the walk out here.

This quiet little 'pause' or break, sitting alone out upon the rocks listening to the water splashing, has made the whole day something extra special. *"Jeg er Fornøyd'"*(I am pleased/content) I have achieved Satori today, in perfect peacefulness.

3:37 PM The message of salvation is the same as getting the message of human love to the person you want to. There is only one, and none other.

The message of the gospel is the same for Jesus.... He has one special person that he wants to tell, how much he loves them......You .

3:45 PM Thinking about when we as men see into the genuine beauty in a woman's heart, through her eyes or her actions and perhaps both, most men's response is to think of affection and love. We almost want to just walk up and give them a hug.

A woman's response toward seeing her mental image of a desirable man is likely the same, or at least similar, if we shed our sometimes arrogant pride long enough to allow them to see into our hearts.

I believe that the reason our feelings are so deeply touched is because, that is the way God wired our hearts and minds. To appreciate the beauty in a woman and the stature in a man, as he, created each to be our companion.

God looks at us, ...each of us *whom he knows he created,* as best I can comprehend it from my human understanding, with the same type of affection that a mother looks at her child to whom she gave birth to, one *whom she knows she 'created'*...... one for whom she will lay down her life in an instant, to save their life, without a moment's hesitation, a second thought, or any regret.

That is the nature of Genuine Love,... gentle and kind, nurturing, unselfish, devoted and faithful. I see that in God's Love for me, His willingness to lay down his life to save me and restore my relationship to himself. When we know that Someone in our personal life, or that God truly loves us, we can know that everything they each do concerning us will always be in our best interest.

.... *Actions Speak Louder Than Words*.....................